Milcreek

POND

By

Kay

Carroll

A dream forever deferred was never one to begin with…

@ @ @ @

To mom… whose love lives on… and
bittersweet memory guides me to pursue my own dream…

Prologue

Her eyes stretched wide open, her temples straining against the pins holding her French ringlets in place to each side of her head. Molly held her teeth firm, begging her limbs not to cringe with the old fear. She leaned forward slightly, but dared not peer from behind her covert hiding place, no matter what.

If she looked and was seen, she might be killed. If she looked and no one was there, she'd die anyway. Ma had always taught Molly not to play around with spirits. "It isn't for us to have nothing to do with what's beyond the naked eye. Those things be under the control of the man upstairs," she'd said. "And I'll have no tom foolery with the man downstairs, not in this house."

Past, present, and future had somehow intertwined in a way she knew was true, but could explain to no one. Looking back, the course began all of four months ago, weaving together early one lingering, worrisome Saturday afternoon.

Life was so much different before then. Not to say it was simpler, or even harder, just different…in a good way… at the time. But then, who can know everything that has happened, what is going on all around us and what is to come.

Like the descendants of Abraham, who knew not what lay in the path ahead, but believed in the promise, that it would be fulfilled.

Chapter One

"Ma, do we have to go now? I told Alex that I would meet him later. Jake can go to town with you when he finishes work, can't he? I wanted to see Alex again. I'm almost 15 years old ma," the frustrated girl moaned, "and I still don't have no regular callers."

Molly stared at her mother...who kept sweeping the floor, while her daughter sulked and pleaded. "Ma-a-a, please, can I stay?" Her mother looked up and shook her head. "Baby you know I wish things were different for us, but we have to do this together. I can't have you sassing me and complaining, I have too much on my mind right now."

"As always," Molly grumbled, grabbing hold of the beat-up spare broom, "get no good reason for nothing."

Molly stamped her foot hard as she could against the brown plank floorboards, slamming the half- worn sweeper bristles against murky dust particles, she could taste in the corners of her mouth and between her teeth, from a week's worth of living. Everything was going wrong! First talk of moving; now she had to go to that backwater town.

All Molly's days seemed to be numbered since her family had to think about leaving Mr. Neuman's farm.

It was just last Sunday that her mother told her they might have to leave for good.   Mr. Neuman was a corn, soy and wheat farmer and the only grain mill owner in the county. Molly's entire family, ma, Jake and her, had worked for him and lived on the Neuman place in this quaint little stone-gray, three room shanty for as long as she could remember. Molly couldn't re-call how she, her mother and brother came to live here, but that didn't matter. She always felt strangely secure with the way she never had to watch how she spoke or how she acted right here—like everywhere else. It was the only life she'd ever known, feeling free of the never-ending limitations of the outside, and she didn't want it to change. Especially now, since Alex...

More straw would be missing from that old broom when ma checked again. She knew it.

Didn't matter. Not much left anyway. A stiff piece flew off and scratched up against her ankle. *Ouch!* She was really going at it. Her mother could get one of the old ones up at the Neuman place, she felt sure, and it'd be same as new.

Ain't fair, she thought, throwing her prized well-practiced diction to the wind.

Molly muttered to herself again, "...never get no darn good reason..."

And the mindful girl wasn't going to ask for one either—at least not from her ma. Molly and her brother Jacob, who everyone knew as Jake, didn't usually ask their mother a lot of questions about why things were the way they were. They just knew that life was the way it was, and they were grateful for their own —on this farm. Their ma did her best and Molly and Jake did what they were told.

It didn't matter how old you got with ma, if she bore you, then you were hers and you did what had to be done, no matter what.

Even Jake, who was almost twenty, didn't question ma. Molly had etched on her brain, both brother and sister submitting to those infuriating weekly inspections.

Molly fell silent. It seemed useless trying to change her mother's mind.

Throwing the battered broom to one side, she dashed off, banging back the well-worn front door on her way out down the long narrow path leading to a quiet familiar place to carefully think things through. She raced along the dirt road past the sodden fields of five neatly kept shanties housing other sharecropper families. Losing steam, she stopped alongside a sunken log-covered cranny, resting her wobbly legs by dropping in her tracks.

The sun bore into her eyes forcing her to squint to see further ahead. Struggling up again, she continued east of the county mill where the trail widened. Her mind still racing, Molly approached the elaborate grounds: including the two-story manor house, six-horse-built stables, a timber-framed barn, another large wood shed and two small whitewashed dwellings beside the house. She settled at the top of the gentle hillside and looked out over the sprawling acreage that made up Mr. Neuman's homestead.

In the distance, she could see familiar waters glistening beyond long branches of tall swaying willows shading the farm. Nearing the little lake, that in her mind she owned, Molly once again fell to her knees while taking in all the splendor of the rambling white-columned house just ahead. With legs folded underneath and arms outstretched, she peered up into the clear blue sky willing the sizzling invisible rays to rid her mind of too much of everything.

July 12, 1879, was a hot summer day. The sun blazed bright—scorching all those living in newly-established Grenada County, Mississippi. So intense it seemed that at any second it might burst and explode in the sky.

On days like these Molly imagined it was winter with rainbow blue, indigo skies sprinkled with cottony clouds and just the right amount of brightness filing through the cold—giving a lavender hue to the blue shimmering waters below. In this space, tall trees, naked without their leaves, stand majestically, shaping the landscape.

Today, however, a frustrated and dejected Molly Elizabeth McCray just squinted into the sun's blinding glare as she pursed her lips in self-pity. Life was changing for her. Maybe this was no time to be yearning for a chance to pass lingering summer days with someone special. Still, she looked down at her glimmering reflection in the water and couldn't help but ponder what she called her "unfortunate existence."

As if the thought of moving wasn't more than enough, she still had to find a way to tell her only likely suitor that there was no way she could meet up with him later that day. It didn't seem to matter to anyone else that he was the only boy who wasn't too scared to come courting her, even though he still couldn't look her in the eye.

"Maybe I should've questioned ma... why, I couldn't stay?" She wondered aloud.

As far as asking her mother to explain things, well, Molly learned long ago that wasn't easy. She really was the only one who got up the "all-fired nerve" to question ma...once in a while. Molly had no idea how she got that way; maybe it was just that she never could get used to doing exactly what she was told in every instance. At times, she'd demand a "doggone" good reason why she had to do something if it didn't seem right to her. Her brother cautioned her that this kind of "gumption," as he called it was going to get her into trouble one day. Still, when it came to speaking her mind, she never paid her brother Jake no-mind.

Molly listened silently to leaves rustling behind her. They belonged to the ripe pecan trees, filled with nuts. The despondent girl stretched out her leg and crushed a few of the fallen pecans under her foot.

"Oh, why couldn't it be a no-count looking day!" she declared with an unladylike spit— aiming for the center of her reflection.

At least, she told herself— getting her mind off her troubles— she was glad this once that none of the sharecropper children showed up for their teaching that day, which she'd taken it upon herself to give them, since few families could spare their children to go to the schoolhouse. Molly gathered the little "urchins" by the lake once every week for her very own take on schooling. Each time they showed up, they positioned their mostly reluctant little frames, just outside of the abundant, arrowhead plants rising out of the shallow water's edge surrounding the pond. The mint green, cream-colored flowery plant's stem tipped in a distinctive arrowhead-shape, reminded Molly of a picture she once saw of a mint julep. She'd seen it on the front cover of a glossy picture book filled with exotic native European plants and flowers, sitting propped on the Neuman's library shelf. But that plant didn't compare to this flower's creamy petals swirling around in clusters of eight, peeking out at her from between the green pointed leaves.

For the last few weeks, she had ended up teaching more nature lessons than she ever planned, which typically started and ended just as soon as an annoying snapping turtle, squawking ducks, or that bothersome muskrat showed up to chomp on what must be some tasty arrowhead tubers. By that time, Molly had completely lost control and almost every child's attention.

A body sure could have used some help by that point.

Something for which she prayed regularly, still waiting for an answer.

Focusing on the tiny ripples the water made, her "courting and moving" dilemma was foremost on her mind, gnawing at her once more.

Staring down, at nothing in particular, Molly's furrowed brow suddenly smoothed.

"Finally," she exhaled loudly.

She bolted upright and dashed around to the opposite side of the pond, past purple swamp milkweeds carrying monarch butterflies sampling its silky nectar, down a widening twig-covered path in the direction of where Jake was working at the mill.

Arriving out of breath, her wavy chestnut hair sticking to her face, she spotted her brother Jake outside the barnhouse-red structure relaxing on a gnarled tree stump with his lunch resting on his lap. The details of her plan fresh in her mind, Molly ran towards him sputtering and pleading, "p-p-please Jake you've gotta help me."

Jacob McCray couldn't help but notice the overly excited state of his unpredictable sister. Not one to make it easy for his rebellious sibling, although he loved her dearly, he let her struggle and plead for a while. He figured a little humble pie would do this one some good.

Little did he know, Molly actually believed this was his chance to show some gumption, along with receiving a tad of her sisterly attention. Besides being good with numbers, and fancying himself a poet, Jake didn't take to doing anything risky. Giving him the opportunity to do something else for a change, she rambled on explaining just how her brother could get into her good graces by accepting his part in her appointed mission.

Much to Molly's surprise, her imagined gift of attention, turned out to be endless begging and swearing-to-do every single, solitary chore of her brother's until the next harvest. So she prattled on and on all through his lunch, weighing him down with her promises until he gave in. Only then, would he finally agree to do her bidding.

"Okay, Okay. I will, I will, but only one thing... do you have to say Milcreek Pond and everything else so proper with your 'ee's and 'ah's?" He paused thoughtfully and then added, "Well, I guess you do...I should too... I reckon."

Exhausted from this unexpected lunch encounter with his trying little sister, Jake rose from the uncomfortable grey stump smoothing back his thick, dark, wavy hair as he stretched to his now full six-foot height. He then made his way back inside to finish a day of work.

According to the plan, as soon as he got off that evening, Jake would meet with an unsuspecting Alex Powton in Molly's place and smooth things over with this so-called fella of hers. Molly would be traveling to town with ma.

****

Molly, relieved that at least this part of her problem was over, became almost lighthearted as she made her way back to the neatly kept little gray shanty she shared with her mother and brother.

She entered the door as her mother was getting out her good yellow hat and fine visiting clothes. Ma always wore her best when they went to town. And she looked pretty in them too, Molly thought. Her long black hair neatly pinned back in a tight chignon, fit perfectly under the narrow-front brimmed, lightly feathered covering.

Molly proudly noticed where the hot summer sun had warmed her mother's skin to a soft golden caramel color. She was convinced of her mother's exceptional good looks.

And it's a wonder too, with what's happened to her...Molly sighed thoughtfully... though pleased at the sight her mother made.

Even though ma was always busy working everyday and didn't talk a lot, she did tell her some things about how hard a time she had as a girl, Molly sadly recalled. Her family possessed a large piece of land at one time. She said that her own "ma", who was part Choctaw Indian, part-African, came to Mississippi by way of Georgia. Her "ma" married her "pa", who was a full-blooded Choctaw, and they were so very blessed and had a good life together—in the beginning. But something happened with a treaty or something and her parents were forced to move with nothing. Times were really terrible and a lot of their people were killed or died, then ma had to go live with another family. Molly didn't know everything that had happened, but ma always got very quiet after that kind of talk.

So Molly didn't push her to tell any more. She sensed that...rarely did anything make ma so very sad.

Now though, as soon as Molly had come through the door, she could tell ma was in her usual good spirits. She told Molly to get cleaned up and wipe the dust off her shoes. Following orders, she went out around back to get water from the pump. Mr. Neuman had the glorious contraption put in a few years before, after ma hurt her back, so they didn't have to go down the road to the community pump used by the other sharecroppers.

As she prepared to wash, cool water emptied into the tin pail. The Neumans are so good to us; Molly thought to herself and smiled. We really don't have no... I mean...any complaints about them, leastways him, being mean or anything like that. That's why I've just got to know why we might have to move on. I'll get up the nerve to ask ma about it on the way to town today, she promised herself, lugging the heavy pail back inside.

Chapter Two

Without fail, at least once a week, the road to "cleanliness is next to godliness" was going to be traveled. Sometimes before school during the week, other times, on weekends. It could be late morning or early afternoon, but always one day or another every single week they got their "going over". This afternoon, without prompting or question, Molly held out her long slim-fingered hands revealing cleanly scrubbed, closely cropped nails, and then lifted high her long wavy tresses for the rest of the regular weekly check. After passing inspection, and strapping on her favorite blue bonnet, Molly and her mother made their way to town, to get, what, she still didn't know.

Since it wasn't too far, just over eight miles, they walked that day as they did most times. Only on days when it was too hot or rainy, did Mr. Neuman let Jake take them to town in the less pretentious second carriage. However, the mill owner just happened to be using it that particular steamy Saturday afternoon.

The Neumans had the two carriages, the great black glossy one with all the fine points that Mrs. Neuman rode in and the plain, much smaller, slate gray one that Mr. Neuman always traveled in to town on business.

Molly recalled the times when Jake would drive ma and her to town on bad weather days— it always caused a bit of a stir. The townspeople resented it when they arrived in that "uppity condition". A term she'd first overheard when their carriage passed a couple walking along the road, on one of their family rainy day outings last summer. Many of the Grenada residents, usually the men, would stop and stare, whipping a few comments at one another, but most never said a word directly to them. Jake suggested to Molly that Mr. Neuman could easily be the richest man in town, so everyone knew better than to say anything to them. Molly wasn't exactly sure what that had to do with anything or how it could possibly make a difference. However, she was just glad to ride to town instead of walking on rainy or very hot summer days.

When sitting near the pond earlier, Molly had clearly hoped for cooler weather, needed all the more now, that she learned Mr. Neuman had the coach today.

The road would be clouded with dust, since it hadn't rained for almost three weeks, causing her to wonder why she had to wipe her black shoes and bathe to go to town in the first place, when they had to walk. She didn't think her patent shoes would look like they had been shined by the time she got to town.

To make matters worse, it was still hot enough today that the usual eight miles felt like twenty-eight . So she didn't think she and ma would look any good when they finally got to there, either.

****

Molly and her mother wearily turned the winding corner from the dirt road onto Main Street, dabbing at their faces with lace cotton handkerchiefs and shaking dust off their dresses. As always, they first stopped in Millville's General Store, a few doors down the way.

Here, ma would regularly get colorful, fancy material for several of Mrs. Neuman's blouses, shawls, and dresses. Once or twice a year, she'd buy plain cloth to add to Molly's few smock-like dresses and Jake's trousers and shirts. This was not their usual week in town so the store owner was stunned to see the comely pair, with shoulders squared, push open the wood framed glass entry door and walk in.

Though looking the proprietor in the eye, at that moment, Molly's mind was on the reason for the day's visit. She'd learned before arriving, while making conversation on the road there, that ma had pushed for her company on this trip to help pick out special sturdy material to make traveling clothes for the move that Molly thought she still didn't know enough about.

The ancient proprietor turned back around, after momentarily searching for some type of distraction, speaking first to ma.

"Hey there Enola...fancy seeing you and little Mo here today. This is sho' a surprise... I don't reckon you come in for 'nother week or two."

"I know Mr. Richmond," ma said. "I needed to pick up material to make some extra things for the children."

"Well ain't you the lucky one, little Mo. Yo' ma here can 'ford to make you extra thangs. Most you chil'run lucky just to have anythang, and you and yo' brother gone git some *extra* thangs," he sneered.

Although the usually snarly Mr. Richmond wasn't looking mean today with his frizzy white hair neatly brushed back, Molly thought, he didn't sound very approving either. His pronounced drawl was sounding even thicker than usual.

What business was it of his why ma wanted to be in the store today? Why do we always have to

answer to folks when we come to town, anyway?
And, I'm nobody's little "Mo,"

Molly never did like old Mr. Richmond. Her dislike started when he first called her, "Lil lap-legged Mo." Now it was just "Mo," but she hated it just the same. Anyway, she was healthy now. Except, she didn't know why sometimes her left foot got real heavy if she was bursting with madness and hurrying to get away from something. Molly wanted no recollection of those memories. So she thought that she had better remember what Jake told her about staying calm.

Purposely looking away from Mr. Richmond's pasty profile, she strained to hold back the scowl she felt pulling on her face.

Molly could hear ma explaining to the frog-faced merchant that they may be doing a bit of traveling in the near future, and that the extra clothes would not be of the frivolous kind. This seemed to finally satisfy the meddlesome man, but he still took ma over to the worn burlap-looking heavier cloth materials kept near the back of the store.

Molly turned and looked around at all the items that had become so familiar to her. Her gaze settled on the glass jars filled with taffy, gumdrops, and honey popcorn balls. She was usually allowed some of those 'sweet delights" on every third visit. Ma used to say they cost too much and would rot Molly's teeth if she got any more than that. Fancying herself a risk taker, Molly was always willing to take that chance, but of course, ma would have none of that. A spindly legged man on an old, wooden cane snail-paced his way to the counter, asking for chewing tobacco, while ma was still picking out cloth. Without hesitation, Mr. Richmond rushed over to help him, long before the man made it over. This gave Molly time to think about what her mother told that nosy "skunk" Mr. Richmond during his intrusive questioning. She said that their family would be taking a "trip" in the near future. A trip, maybe that's all it really was. Molly probably heard wrong, when she thought ma said they might have to move on. It was just going to be a trip. They were going to visit some folks, maybe kinfolk they'd never seen before. They probably wrote ma and asked her to come and visit for a while, Molly thought as she tried to convince herself.

After leaving the general store, mother and daughter headed to the boardinghouse up the road. Molly's mother had been checking there for over six months for extra work on Saturday. Crossing over, they spotted and gave their regards to two of their sharecropper neighbors who were in town that day hauling handmade goods to sell in the town square. Following up once more at the boardinghouse and getting the same answer again, they headed back to the farm.

As they were leaving, the manager called out to ma, "There is generally a rush of strangers and widowers needing rooms in the fall and winter...come back then."

Walking back home, tall forest green pines lined their path as they approached bright open flatlands littered with crops, pasture, and a grassy meadow filled with wildflowers.

Since the sun didn't seem so high in the sky now, with the clouds blanketing part of its intense brightness, it felt a lot cooler.

****

Molly couldn't stop thinking of why her family would have to move on. If they really did have to, she wasn't so sure. Maybe ma was sick, she wondered, lagging behind her mother who moved a few steps ahead.

"Oh, yes", Molly softly cried out, as she expertly snapped her fingers, remembering the talk she and ma had last week that had given her a notion that something was wrong.

It was last Tuesday, when ma slipped on some corn husk on the ground outside the Neuman's barn. At that time, Molly told her that she didn't know what she would do if something happened to her. Ma's response scared her something awful at first, but then made her think about a thing or two.

"Baby," her ma said, "You can always talk to family. It don't matter if they're here or gone."

"How's that…?" Molly questioned the possibility.

"In your dreams…you can visit and never have to go a day without seeing your ma, even once I'm gone on."

Molly wasn't so sure that she could or would even want to do that. And that kind of talk was not the same kind of moving, of a bodily sort, she wanted to talk about. Anyway, ma was always talking about spirits and all.

Dismissing that chilly thought, another possibility clicked in Molly's head. Maybe they had no money! But it didn't seem that they needed much money to live the way they were. Ma got some wages for working in the Neuman's house during the week, and they didn't have to buy food or pay for a place to live.

But sometimes, if ma wanted them both to have a pretty dress, or a nice shirt and pants for Jake, she would have to save a long time to get the material from Mr. Richmond.

"That's it... THAT'S IT!" Molly repeated piercingly, startling her mother who stumbled, stiffened, and turned towards her daughter who had fallen almost ten paces behind.

Molly grinned knowingly at her, running to catch up, believing she'd figured out her mother's well kept secret.

Ma wants more money.

She cautiously whispered in her mind with her mother still staring at her. That's why she was trying for that rooming house job in town. If she can get that job we won't have to move on, Molly thoughtfully convinced herself, latching arms with her mother, now willing to keep-up.

Chapter Three

Back from the mill and his meeting with Alex, Jake was sitting at the kitchen table when his mother and sister arrived home. Like a bull, Molly charged at him demanding details.

"Well, come on tell me, what did he say? Jake, what did Alex say when you told him?" She cried, giving her brother no time to answer, grabbing at his sleeve and almost knocking over his bowl of hot stew.

"Hold on now girl. I just told him what you said," Jake answered as he loosened his sister's grip.

"I told him that you really wanted to meet him today at that lake of yours, but you had to go with ma.

"He really didn't say nothing much. Just 'okay' and would like me to go fishing with him sometime."

"Fishing?! Did he say that he would like to meet me tomorrow?" Molly insisted on knowing.

"Didn't you remember to ask? I bet you didn't even ask him! I told you to tell him that I could meet him tomorrow at the same spot on Milcreek Pond or down the road from Mr. Neuman's, if he couldn't make it there. Did you forget?"

"Oh yeah, now I remember," Jake said, taking his time. "I did tell him that you could meet him tomorrow, but I don't recollect him saying whether or not he wanted to meet you."

"Anyway Molly," he continued, "you need to slow down." Jake paused to give her a chance to do just that.

"Look at your face, it's all red," he pointed out.

"Hold your breath, catch it or whatever it is you do, and listen. Now, a fellow don't take too kindly to a pushy gal, so I've heard. So, don't be in such an all-fired hurry to get this fellow to court you regularly. Give him some time and if he likes you, he'll come around again, real soon."

Molly listened all right, but she didn't like what she was hearing. She was not one to wait for something that she was so close to getting, but might get away. If she could have just met Alex today, she wouldn't have to listen to this sermon on how to be a proper lady-in-waiting.

And what was so wrong with her trying. She would keep on, too! But Jake didn't have to worry; Molly wouldn't wear herself ragged trying to get that boy's attention. She'd rather be an old maid than be seen as a desperate female.

Molly could feel a hateful scowl pulling on the left side of her face. She forced the corners of her mouth into a thin straight line, and told herself to shock her brother by holding her tongue, at least this time.

Determined to respond gratefully, she replied, "Thanks for toting the message, big brother. As they say in these here parts, 'I'm much obliged to ya.'"

Jake laughed watching his sister sashay into the back room like a southern Queen Victoria, coupled with her obvious attempt to be overly ingratiating. Everyone knew she never talked that way anymore.

As Molly took off her good clothes, she decided her Alex worries had to wait until tomorrow. She had too many things filling up her cluttered brain, which demanded that she lay them to rest along with putting her feet up for the night.

****

The next morning, Molly took up precisely where she'd left off. After a hearty breakfast, following her mother's lead, Molly hummed her way into the big sleeping room to help make the beds.

The area was partitioned off into two parts— the larger one for ma and Molly, and the smaller for her brother Jake. They whipped and tucked sheets, made crisper, after Molly threw open the shutters to let in the fresh morning air.

Building up her nerve, Molly breathed in the pungent scent of the morning dew mingled with the smell of livestock and was poised— determined to do something she usually never did.

"Ma," she began, "you remember last week when we were outside tending the chickens, and you said that we may have to move on soon?" Molly hurried on before her mother could respond, "I've been thinking about it a whole lot since then. And on yesterday, while we were in town, you asked at the boardinghouse just like you've been the last few months about work on Saturday. Well, I was just thinking that how if we have to move on, can you work at that place? And if you did get the job there, does that mean we won't have to move?"

Molly forged on a bit nervously. But then, maybe I heard you wrong and that you didn't say that we would actually have to move, or at least not for a long time, anyway." She stopped to take a breath and get more nerve.

In that instant, Molly witnessed her mother's warm eyes become veiled, then close slightly.

Ever-cautious Enola listened to her daughter's hurried speech in silence. As Molly pressed on, she looked away and then back at the anxious girl, letting her babble.

"I know that Jake says that I talk too much, but I was thinking that this time I wasn't talking too much, but trying to get something straight, that's all."

Silent for a moment, her eyes pleaded for assurance that she had not made a mistake in questioning her mother.

"I'm asking why, ma, just this one time?"

"Molly," Enola abruptly silenced her, "you know your brother is right, you do talk too much, way too much. I just pray that all your prattle don't cause you a lot of trouble one day."

And that was the end of that.

Chapter Four

As sizzling summer days moved towards much milder autumn afternoons, there was no more talk from ma about possibly moving. Molly took that as a definite sign that things had gotten settled once and for all. Whatever the mysterious reason was that her secretive mother had to bring up the subject in the first place; it was not a good one anymore.

Molly strolled home from the schoolhouse that afternoon with thoughts of the annual Autumn Festival coming up in late October. With everything else on her mind, she'd almost forgotten. Now that she was coming up on fifteen years, she had hoped that she could go and that good-looking Alex was still interested enough to ask her. He had come around three times since that day she stood him up over the summer.

Well, *I didn't actually stand him up; I did send Jake in my place.*

Molly's hopeful thoughts were interrupted by the sight of Mr. Neuman riding up the road.

"Well... good afternoon, Molly," he called to her.

She answered respectfully, "Good afternoon, sir."

He smiled down from his coach, "You sure are growing up to be quite the lovely young lady."

Molly was at ease since she had always felt incredibly relaxed around the friendly mill owner whom she'd known all her life.

"Thank you, sir," she continued, "I am old enough now to help ma out at the house. She said that she might start bringing me next week to serve at some of the luncheons and dinners."

Molly stopped to take a deep breath. Ma had suggested she try this to stop her from rambling on and on and such, she recalled.

"That would be fine Molly, but aren't you in school during the week?"

"Oh yes, sir, but only until noon, since it's summer and this is my last year. Anyway, I'm almost fifteen now, I pretty much know everything there is to know. Mr. Temple, my teacher, says that he's had enough of me trying to correct him in front of the class. He says he's sure that I must know more about arithmetic, history, and reading than he does," Molly replied, almost forgetting to stop for breath.

Mr. Neuman laughed. "And I just bet you might be that smart, Molly."

He remembered her mother once "declared" wearily that Molly was the most talkative and know-it-all child she'd ever laid eyes on.

"Well, yes, since you are finished with school so early in the day," he offered, "I'm sure Mrs. Neuman would look forward to your helping out around the place. There must be plenty of extra chores that you can do."

At the mention of Mrs. Neuman, Molly felt a slight chill run through her. Although she was grateful to her, the lady of the house made no secret that Molly, her mother, and brother, were not very welcome on "her" family's farm. Mr. Neuman didn't know this, of course, since his wife always spoke so kindly whenever he was in earshot.

Bet most folks don't know the Mrs. Neuman that I get to see.

Molly's mind wandered.

It's almost like she was two different people. Whenever I see her going to her big shiny carriage, or strolling in her garden looking so perfect and always in fashion, I always say, "Good morning, madam" but she never says anything back. She just stares at me. Then sometimes she won't look at me at all.

When Molly was very young, she thought Mrs. Neuman acted that way because somehow she found her strange or homely. Most of the share-croppers said the girl was quite pretty, even love-ly, like her mother. With such comments, as she grew into a teenager, Molly began to wonder even more why most of the "fellas" didn't even try to talk to her, much less come courting.

Molly once overheard some old folks whisper-ing about her "supposing to have something that they are scared of," but for the life of the girl, she didn't know what it could be.

"Who would be afraid of me?" she had pon-dered aloud.

Molly didn't fancy herself to be a breathtaking beauty like ma, or even Mrs. Neuman, she hated to admit. But what stared back at Molly from the looking glass wasn't so bad, she believed.

To see for herself, a few times, she'd snuck into one of the guest bedrooms at the Neuman's and peered into their looking-glass. She didn't hate what she saw. Staring back at her was an oval face framing wide-set almond-shaped eyes, a slightly upturned nose, and a full wide set mouth that was maybe too wide, according to ma and Jake.

Long wavy chestnut brown plaits hung down below her waist. Her skin shone of ripe peaches mingled with creamy buttercup. Someone had once given her the nickname "peaches and cream." Her neck, long and graceful, and her waist was small. They complimented long lean

legs that came from all the walking, she suspected.   The last time she'd looked, Molly noticed
she'd finally developed a nice roundness to her
slim, fairly tall frame.

Convinced she couldn't scare anyone, Molly
invoked   "Ma's rule" which had always taught
Molly that no matter what, "God never gave nobody no good reason to be evil to no one."

So how could Mrs. Neuman act so mean to
her? Thinking that maybe Mrs. Neuman was
crazy or something, Molly laughed to herself.

With a smile still on her face, Molly pushed
aside her streaming thoughts long enough to
graciously respond to Mr. Neuman's acceptance
of her original offer, "That would be just grand.
Thank you so much, sir. I sure would be happy
to help out at the house and earn a bit, too."

Mr. Neuman wished Molly a final good afternoon, after reassuring her that she would be welcome at the house.   He then stepped into his
stately carriage, bid her goodbye, and rode off
down the road to town. Molly watched the coach
as it drove off with the kind gentleman she'd
grown so accustomed to.

Just as quickly, her wayward thoughts turned
to Alex and the upcoming Autumn Festival
which now took on new meaning for her. She pictured her self-appointed beau next to her in his
suit, lean and tall, dark hair combed back, steel
grey eyes, and a chiseled jaw.

Already, plans were whirling around in Molly's
head.   She couldn't help but sound off the things

she could get and how she planned to shine—
thanks to weekly wages from this newfound position up at the Neuman-house.

Chapter Five

Now that she was almost fifteen, Molly could go to dances that were held at night for older folks. That would be the best part of working at the house now; she'd told everyone who would listen. Molly would be getting enough money to buy material for a new dress to wear to the festival in just under two months. That's all she could think about while she worked. Molly knew that she would barely be able contain her excitement from the beginning.

It wasn't so important to have a new dress for those "ole barn dances." But now that she would have a beau who would be courting her with ballroom dancing and all— well… that old dress ma regularly let out just would not do.

Most of all, Molly had almost perfected learning to talk the way ma had been teaching her. Her mother said that it didn't matter that everyone else talked in some way like ole' Mr. Richmond. But that her own "ma" taught her to talk proper-like, and she was teaching Molly and her brother to do the same with no "yes-m's" and "naw's" and the like. Only, sometimes Molly would go back and forth.

But now, she thought, "I am talking proper almost all the time. No amount of training, though, would ever stop me from saying, 'ma.' Nothing else feels right. 'Ma' will always be 'ma.'"

Her mother said the proper talk would help her, especially if she decided to be a teacher. Since everyone told her she talks too much about anything and everything, the idea of her being a teacher wasn't so far-fetched.

Ma said that if she got even more schooling, at a higher level they call it, she would be able to teach highly educated folks too. Not just the young ones she'd been helping on Mr. Neuman's place and the neighboring farms.

With so many thoughts racing through her mind, Molly fell into a brisk pace on her walk home. She knew her usual chores would be waiting and her final lessons on how to talk properly would have to be reviewed with ma at lunch. Molly would have preferred to wait for the lessons, but ma had to go back to work at the Neuman house after lunch.

Molly arrived home before her mother and was preparing sandwiches for lunch when she walked in.

"Are you here all day now, Molly?" her mother asked.

"Yes ma, remember, my teacher, Mr. Temple said he was going to start me on half days this month, since I seem to be such an 'intellectual' as he puts it. I don't know if he is trying to say something nice or making fun. I can't help it. Thanks to you, I sometimes know more than he does," Molly said matter-of-factly.

"Just hold on a minute, let's not get too big for our breeches little lady," her mother chided. "You have to remember that you can be smart without telling every person you meet up with just how bright you are. People don't want to be made to feel that you think you're better than them."

"Oh, ma, that hurts. You know I'm not like that. I'm nice to everybody. I only like to talk. And things, well they just come out," she shrugged, then set the sandwiches on the kitchen table.

"Well, that's one reason why I keep telling you not to talk so much. I know you don't mean no harm, but too much talk always gets our kind into trouble. You must move yourself up slow and quiet-like in this big 'ole world here," her mother cautioned her.

"I'm trying ma. But sometimes I just feel so good inside; it's so burdensome always trying to hide it. But anyway, I'm all ready for my proper lessons this afternoon. I think I only need a few more, and then everyone at the Autumn Festival will see just how grownup and proper I am." Molly almost squealed, trying to contain her enthusiasm, while mouthing the long "ee" and short "o" sounds she'd practiced all summer.

"Girl, I must say you have mastered the art of talking proper real well, even better than your own "ma," she conceded. "I think you picked up a lot from being around Mr. Neuman's children before they went up North to finish school. And it's good that nobody around here minds us talking proper. You know some places the townspeople get really mad about folks like us talking good English," her mother added, "But what's this about the Autumn Festival—you expecting to go this year?"

"Why of course, ma. I'm fourteen going on fifteen now, did you forget?" Molly questioned accusingly.

"How could I?" her mother laughed. "But Jake didn't go to that function until he was going on seventeen."

"Oh ma, that's how it is with boys, they never want to go. They don't even want to go when they're eighteen. Why, if they could, they'd wait until they were twenty-five. I think it's because they have to dress up and dance and all." Molly added. "You remember, Jake was never too big on dancing proper and wearing fine clothes. He'd just as soon go out, mount a horse, and kick up dust all afternoon. It wasn't until that last time at the festival that he started to enjoy himself."

Molly's mother listened as she finished her sandwich, then offered, "Well, I guess I could let your party dress out a few inches, but I think this is the last time we'll be able to stretch it."

"That's something else I wanted to talk to you about." Molly paused, wondering exactly how to put it. "Uh, Uh, I can't wear that old relic to the festival. It was okay for the barn dances when I was eleven or twelve, but for an occasion like this, no. I think this calls for something new, something blue, and something soft and bright— like the color of the Mississippi river in the noon sunshine."

Slowly getting up from the sawbuck table, ma quipped, "Molly, I don't know nothing about sunshine and river water, and for sure don't know what in heaven an "old relic" is, but I do know that I don't have money for cloth to make a new party dress for you."

Molly followed her mother over to the brown washing tub, "I know, that's why I did not say I wanted you to give me any money for yard goods. I decided to earn it myself."

Her mother stopped rinsing the plates and turned around. "And how, pray-tell, will you do that?"

"Well, I saw Mr. Neuman today and he wants me to work for him, and..." sputtered Molly with excitement.

"Wait a minute, slow down girl," her mother interrupted.

"What'd you mean work for him?" She questioned, sitting back down at the kitchen table.

"You see, ma," Molly detailed the conversation with Mr. Neuman from earlier that afternoon, then added, "He said I would get paid for it and I didn't even ask, not once. Ma, I didn't even go on and on this time, talking too much. I caught my breath like you said."

With a level gaze, the woman was silent as she studied her lovely, determined daughter.

"Molly, I could use help at the house, that's for sure, but I never thought that Mr. Neuman would offer you a job helping me out. Well, that's fine. I think that would work out. But I don't know if you can make enough money to get material in time to finish a party dress before the festival," her mother confided.

"Still, I will do all I can to help you since you really could use the new dress.

I think I may be getting as anxious as you, my girl. I can remember the times I used to dance at those goings-on," she added.

Molly watched as her mother got that far-away look in her eyes that sometimes came when she reflected on the rare "good times." As always, at those moments, Molly smiled lovingly at her "ma."

Giving her time to recollect, Molly rose quietly and went over to finish rinsing the plates.

Both mother and daughter had forgotten the talking lessons for that day.

Chapter Six

Molly had been helping out in the late afternoon and evenings up at the Neuman house for a week now. Her job was to help her mother with the dusting and polishing, turning down the beds in the evening, and serving the late lunches and dinners. Because of her bad back, Enola never did any of the heavy work, like scrubbing the floors, or washing the clothes. She hurt it a few years earlier trying to move the Maplewood cabinet in the Neuman's drawing room, so she could sweep behind it. Mr. and Mrs. Neuman took that into consideration when giving her new duties.

Even while working, Molly and her mother were always given plenty of time to have their own lunch and dinner. They were never allowed, however, in the formal blue-draperied dining room, much to Molly's dismay. They would pass through the long hallway to eat in the large, bay-windowed corner of the soft-yellow and mahogany, wood kitchen.

Sometimes when Mrs. Neuman was out at one of her many charity affairs, Mr. Neuman would have lunch in the breakfast corner with Molly and her mother. Those times together were a bit out of the ordinary, but that's why she always enjoyed them.

"Molly, I hope you haven't gotten into any trouble since you've been here this week," Mr. Neuman teased.

"Why no, sir," she responded soberly.

"I just do what I always do when I finish helping ma here. I go home and make sure Jake has not come in and messed up everything I washed and straightened up before I left that morning. He's a top notch brother, I'd swear by this to anyone, but he leaves a trail of destruction behind him—at least at our place he does. After I'm finished picking up after him, there is no time left to do my own chores."

She paused. "But yesterday, I began working on something of my own, something a little different."

"Oh?" the mill owner smiled, questioning her serious expression with his raised brow. "And what would that be?"

"Uh-uh, Mr. Neuman sir," she shook her head to emphasize her point, "I couldn't possibly tell you. I want everyone to be surprised.

"And when will we all learn of this big surprise?" He asked with genuine interest.

"Now, if I tell you that sir, I would be giving it away. There wouldn't be much left to my surprise." Everyone will be shocked, though. I can tell you that much! No…amazed. Yes, that's what they'll be," Molly declared with an intent gaze.

As if on-cue, Walter Neuman continued his questioning and looked at ma, hoping to get some type of hint. "Enola, now I know you have some idea what this great surprise is all about," he said.

Ma held his gaze with a slight smirk and a raised eyebrow. "Now Mr. Neuman, you know that wouldn't be fair to my Molly, if I was to let you have some idea of what her surprise was. I hope you understand, sir?"

"Do I have any choice?" He grinned and raised both hands in mock surrender. "But Molly, don't let it be too big of a shock for us. You know we're not all as young as you. We may not be able to take all the excitement."

"Yes sir," Molly blushed shyly, surprisingly short on words for once.

The adults continued talking about the usual town matters like hopes to rebuild the old half demolished Grenada Railroad depot. The trains still stopped at the usual platform, but the first station was destroyed by the Union Calvary over 15 years ago, and the Illinois Central Railway folks were planning to rebuild on the existing site one day soon.

Before Mr. Neuman and ma rose at the same time, and eased their refreshed limbs from under breakfast corner table with ma stopping to clean-up, their duties leading them to go in opposite directions; Molly secretly wished things could be this way— always.

Sitting back, the soft breeze drifted through the bay window and the gentle sway of the willow-oak branches in the early afternoon lulled all past thoughts far away from her mind. She lingered a few moments longer, and was strangely comforted by the lonely wail of a railroad train whistle in the distance—both escaping the present.

Chapter Seven

Spring 1859

Walter Neuman came directly from Germany to America looking for a better life. He'd followed his much older half- brother who'd come over more than twenty-five years earlier; the first of the Neuman's to arrive, making a place for himself, before dying of influenza two years prior. Walter's second stop was on the shores of North Carolina where he made his way west to the Mississippi. At 23, he worked hard and prided himself on protecting the somewhat substantial means he'd brought with him. In his travels, Walter felt fortunate to come across a large piece of rich abandoned land in an area that would one day be known as Grenada County. Town legend had it deserted years earlier by an ousted religious group that was forced to leave the land they'd first claimed. Walter believed himself to be the last man to wish bad luck on anyone, but he would take good fortune wherever he could find it.

The newcomer discovered that according to the law of the land, he had to develop the acreage and work it for one year for it to belong to him free and clear.

At once he set his mind to try to make something of the neglected property. He didn't get much support from the towns' residents, though. They considered him to be an outsider, one of the new crop of German and Swiss folks coming to what they called the "New World." The townspeople figured those folks had no good reason to leave their own homeland. Things weren't too bad over there from what they'd heard. In addition, when it came to Neuman, many people felt, "He don't seem to take to the ways of us townfolk. We fought hard to get and keep what we got."

For most of the plantation owners and farmers, land included well over three-hundred acres with horses, cattle and oxen. Visitors might see horse-powered threshing or plowing with oxen. Most crops relied on a large slave workforce. The crop-covered fields included cotton, tobacco, corn, oats, and sugarcane; as well as wheat, vegetables, and grasses. In most houses, women cooked and practiced their crafts—making straw hats and soap. Nature trails ran along the Mississippi river through acres and acres of woods and prairie. Poorer farmers were fighting for more rights, along with more favorable social and economic conditions.

During this time, Walter's days were long and tedious, but rewarding. He set out to build himself a fine, sturdy house and persevered to make a good livelihood. He was determined that with or without help, he wasn't moving on nor was he going back 'home.'

Since he had come prepared, Walter was able to use a portion of the sizeable amount of money he'd brought with him to America. He decided to use a bit of it to pay some of the more willing men to haul the materials required to build the house he wanted— not just needed. In Germany, Walter and his family had been accused of having "too-big dreams." Being confident and self-assured, he saw no reason to refute that account of himself now.

****

It took about eight months of everyone working day and night to get the showplace Walter wanted. He stood proudly outside of the gleaming, Greek Revival house which he hoped would be filled with a wife and many children in no time.

While building his home, Walter had hired some of the ostracized townspeople. The locals called them Indians. They helped him begin his large wheat and corn crops. Since many of the other farmers were growing cotton, he thought he'd carve out his own niche.

Walter felt that with the extensive knowledge of technology and design learned in trade schools in Hamburg; he could develop plans for a large mill to process not only his own crops, but that of any other grains and cereals other local farmers grew. He knew of no other large mill of this type within three states.

Walter managed to purchase 500 additional acres in that year, so he decided to build the mill less than a half-mile east of his stately home. It included land bordering a small local lake the townspeople strangely had referred to only as "haunted." Walter was never superstitious, nor was he willing to listen to tales from those who were. He'd decided the lake was more than large enough to accommodate his needs and would allow for the proper drainage. He gave it a new name and a new lease on life.

As the building of Walter's state-of-the-art mill was progressing, with the help of heavy machinery, and all of the townspeople, and Choctaw Indians he could hire; he took Sundays' off for a bit of time to get to know the people of this remote little town. If he was ever to get married and have a family, he thought he'd better get to it.

After a year, the townspeople still considered the new stranger in town an outsider. Although they were quick to see what a fine catch he would be for their unhitched young daughters, they still worried. They wagged on about how anyone with the means to build such a fine house, start a tremendous corn and wheat crop, and not to mention what was sure to be the biggest and best mill in the South, must be a wealthy man. Although... they felt he took great pains to act as if he were not like the rest of them. Even those who figured him to be "crazy as a loon," could see that the fine, strapping German was building himself some kind of showplace—like the ones they'd heard about up in the state of Virginia. Many whispered that he might even be the best catch in this or any other county.

For this reason, they softened their view of the stranger. Although they still didn't like his ways with the Indians and the free ones. It was true; folks had never seen the likes of someone like him and doubted that they would ever again.

****

After pondering his new mission to start a family, that Sunday morning Walter walked into the large yellow brick and cedar Wilshire Southern Baptist Church, 20 minutes late for service. The arched entrance of the well-built church seemed to provide the perfect framework for all to view the newcomer in his Sunday finest. Every head turned to take in the towering six-foot-two man with wavy golden hair and fiery blue eyes. His well -defined muscular build, obvious even through his parted overcoat, prompted the women to look a bit longer than was customary. Walter walked up the middle of the sanctuary and took one of the few open seats near the front next to a family he recognized from his daily forays to town.

Ignoring the momentary disruption, the reverend cleared his throat and continued on with his sermon. Then the man sitting next to Walter turned and not-so-quietly introduced himself, his wife, and children. Walter smiled and politely nodded his head in acknowledgement. He became uncomfortably aware of the reverend's growing displeasure at the interruption and tried to remain as immobile and attentive as possible, despite feeling that all eyes were on him.

The sermon continued on with the usual topic, which most know: "Treat Thy Neighbor As Thyself." From what he could tell of some of the townspeople, few put those words into practice, Walter thought. While sitting and listening, he wondered how a message like this one struck the people sitting here in the church. From his understanding many of them owned or would like to own slaves to do all the work for them, even in their houses. For that reason, the Choctaw Indians that Walter employed to build and help maintain his farm were extremely grateful for an honest day's work.

Walter knew from what his workers told him, that this was how life was in many different parts of America. They said, "...just wouldn't be seemly if everyone was to be treated equal," and they didn't think anyone ever felt that the Good Book meant "everyone." Besides, "no one thought much about it, just listening to a good Sunday sermon."

Before coming to America, Walter had learned how to write and speak a bit of English early in his childhood. By the time he'd arrived here, he was quite fluent. But there were times, as when leaving the church today and finding every un-married female over age 13 pointing in his direc-tion, that Walter wished he had a very limited understanding of the language.

"Why hello again, Neuman. Lovely day isn't it?"

Standing directly behind Walter was the man who'd introduced himself and his family while in church. Seemingly familiar, he reminded Walter that they'd met several months ago at a town meeting. Walter also recalled riding past his large, but unfortunately run-down farm at the edge of his own property.

Hugh Jackson's land made an impression on Walter the first week he entered the town less than a year ago. Walter had heard that Jackson had three daughters, and was dying to marry two of them off. Walter had met up with the father a few times when in town for supplies. Looking more closely at the man, Walter saw how worn

Jackson appeared, possibly because he was trying to run a farm on his own without the help of a son-in-law or even a prospect of one. Walter remembered that one of the Choctaws working on his house mentioning that years ago Jackson's land was thriving. But it was rumored that Jackson drank up most of the profits he made over the years, leaving him with little to invest in the upkeep of the place.

"Yes, it is a glorious afternoon," Mr. Jackson. Walter commented, determined to give this unfortunate gentleman all of his attention. "And please call me Walt," he tried to sound pleasant, "We've been neighbors for many months now."

Walter thought it best to be on good, if not familiar, terms with everyone he encountered. He never knew who might be available to lend a hand in a place where one had no relations to count on, and because that was his way. Keeping this in mind, he appeared to happily endure what he knew was sure to come next.

"Why yes, I sure will do that, Walt. I believe you've met the missus and my oldest girls, Jean and Marie, inside?"

"Yes, Mr. Jackson, I do believe I've had the pleasure. Good afternoon, once more ladies, how charming all of you look on this fine day," Walter smiled, tipping his hat and nodding to each of the women, while expertly placing the daughters ages at around 20 and 22.

Jackson's daughters blushed before casting their eyes down, but not before both had taken in every aspect of Walter's youthful, handsome appearance.

Since Mr. Jackson was at least twenty-five years Walter's senior, he didn't wonder why Jackson didn't ask Walter to address him by his first name. In addition, the eligible bachelor was well aware of Jackson's goal to align Walter to the generation of his hopelessly lackluster-looking eldest daughter.

After exchanging the expected pleasantries, Walter hoped beyond hope that he could get away with just enough gallantry.

"Why what a wonderful way you have with words," the wife now began, killing his hopes. "We would love to have you over for dinner this afternoon. It would give our family a chance to get to know you a bit better and you can tell us all about your country. Please say you can come, Mr. Neuman."

"That would be wonderful, madam, but I have quite a bit of work to do today. A fence needs mending very badly," he said apologetically.

"Well, how about next Sunday," she quickly retort-ed.

Noticing each daughter's eyes fixed on him and eagerly awaiting his response, Walter took his time trying to think of another excuse that would get him out of this. But before he could open his mouth, the wife accepted the invitation for him.

"Well then, it's settled Mr. Neuman. We will look for you at three o'clock next Sunday."

Talk about being railroaded, Walter thought. He had barely looked at any of the daughters, much less said a word to them. But he knew he had seen enough, and now he was stuck with an unwanted dinner engagement for which he had no time.

"Well, I guess I can't say that I didn't know it was coming," he said under his breath.

"Yes, young man, did you say something," the wife asked.

"Yes madam." Walter responded gallantly, "As you said, next Sunday at three o'clock would be splendid, truly splendid."

After exchanging a few more good-natured remarks with the family, Walter bid the tiresome group goodbye and promised to arrive promptly for dinner.

Riding back to his home, he looked out over the countryside— a mixture of low-rolling hills and fertile flatland— and pondered the many purchases he still needed to make. Although he did make a splendid sight riding horseback, Walter had argued with himself about getting a small sturdy coach. He didn't think he needed one a few months back, but looking toward the future, it may be the right time. After all, he was moving up in status and considering a life with more than just himself in it. The Gilbertson Stagecoach Company was over in the next town. He'd stop in there before the week was out.

Almost home—passing through rows of long-leaf pine trees alongside both sides of the road—

Walter thought about the message given in church today. Despite the prevailing views on equality, he knew that there were those in town who actually *did* believe that the "Good Book's" neighbor referred to *all* people. He knew some did everything they could to act it out, even going so far as to sacrifice their own livelihoods and even their lives to bring about change.

As Walter exited the generous stables he had built to house up to six horses, he though again about possibly buying a coach.

Striding across the rolling green lawn in the making, Walter cringed as he remembered what was in store for him next Sunday—dinner with the Jacksons. He hoped that evening didn't drag on so long that he did not have the chance to get back and truly enjoy his day of rest.

But today, he'd allotted his afternoon for the fence mending project he'd mentioned to the Jacksons, just a while ago outside church.

After rounding up chickens he'd found roaming around the farm yesterday, he could not afford to have any more hens getting through those four openings.

As Walter kicked the dust off his shoes and entered his house, he felt a warm sense of security that he had lost these last few weeks. Things were beginning to look up now that he knew that in just over a month, the original property would actually belong to no one but him completely free and clear.

Chapter Eight

Inside, Ciaok was working to prepare lunch. Walter hired him to do some of the domestic work that he didn't have time to tackle and it turned out that he was also an excellent cook. Over these few months, Ciaok and Walter had become close companions to the dismay of much of the neighboring townspeople. Since they spent so many hours together, during this time, Ciaok told Walter about his past.

As the landowner made his way up the specially designed curved staircase in the center of the large entry hall, he wondered about Ciaok's future there. The young Indian mentioned only the week before that it would be best for him to make his way up North before the year was out, which caught his employer and friend by surprise.

Walter moved past the doorway of his large master bedroom suite. As he took off and hung up his overcoat, he wondered if any amount of pay could keep his trusted employee there with him. It seemed that Ciaok's people had been through so much hardship and he had so many haunting memories involving this part of the country. That's why he just wanted to be somewhere else. Ciaok confided that no place was better than any other for his people, but he just needed a change.

Walter walked into his sitting area, past the striped wing chair, and seated himself on the settee in front of the green-draped windows. He liked the look of the mahogany four-poster bed which sat directly across from the open window and received just the right amount of sunlight to wake him early each morning.

Walter had developed the habit of getting up at sunrise, which was necessary for survival if he was to make it in these parts. He recalled the first morning in his house. Walter woke with the light streaming on his face and Ciaok at his bedside with a breakfast tray in hand filled with eggs, toast, bacon, and coffee. Walter, who was not used to breakfast in bed, especially such an elaborate meal, directed Ciaok back downstairs into the kitchen. To Ciaok's surprise, Walter followed

shortly thereafter, insisting that the trusted employee take half of the meal and share it with
him.

Ciaok had been in Walter's employ for only
three months now, but had already developed a
feel for just how different Walter Neuman was
from the rest of the townspeople and for that
matter anyone he'd ever met. When the young
German had questioned Ciaok's qualifications for
manservant, he'd also inquired about Ciaok's
past.

With great pain, over the months, the young
man recounted the history that had been passed
down to him from his grandfather. This is how
the story began: "The white man had good reason to hold out the hand of friendship to the
Choctaw. Our people were the go-between for
the United States and the Spanish and French in
the Southeast and the Old Southwest. Once the
Spanish and French left, the Choctaw were no
longer needed as peacemakers, and land-hungry
white settlers came for the rich Choctaw farms.
Our lives grew worse when Mississippi became a
territory and then unbearable when it became a
state."

As Ciaok continued, Walter seemed to be
amazed that someone so young could have
moved around so much. Any other landowner in
town could have told the young newcomer that
this way of life was commonplace for Ciaok's
people.

Looking back, the young Indian remembered the first day he and members of his now small tribe had decided to approach Mr. Walter Neuman about work on his new farm. They expected the usual ill-tempered demeanor and perfunctory "no," which had become commonplace. So when the man stood staring at Ciaok and the others for what seemed like a lifetime, he felt sure that they would be sent away. But the accepting stranger agreed to hire everyone in the group. He even asked if they knew any other skilled workers, like themselves, who were looking for work. The offer they received that day moved many of them to tears. Never before had Ciaok encountered such a response. From that moment on, although younger, Walter Neuman became someone that Ciaok looked up to and trusted. Many times, since then, the now appreciative manservant confided in Walter, yet he was obviously pondering a possible journey up North.

Now changed into work clothes, Walter opened his bedroom door to encounter unfamiliar voices coming up from the entry hall.

"Hell n-no, it can't be," he hollered with exasperation, recognizing one of the voices.

"What in the world? It can't be! How does that Jackson turn up at my door uninvited? Didn't I just leave that fellow only an hour ago, telling him I had work to do?" He muttered a string of questions to himself.

This was an unexpected follow-up visit that Walter felt he could surely do without. Especially considering Mr. Jackson was accompanied by his daughters, Walter noted as he'd slipped from his bedroom and peered downstairs. And there was also one other person down there that Walter had never seen before.

With their backs toward him, Walter was able to position himself over the balcony railing to see perfectly into the entry hall without being seen. He noted that the young lady with them seemed to be more polished than the two sisters. She had an air of distinction about her that suggested that she might be from Boston, maybe Maryland or somewhere in the Northeast. Although he settled in the South, Walter had learned the ways of and had great respect for most Northerners.

He knew the North to have always been busier, and seemingly more supportive of entrepreneurism. The economy of New England, and the upper middle states was, up to this time, dominated by overseas shipping and agriculture. Now they were moving towards manufacturing and technology he'd heard. Northerners created the Erie Canal, from the ocean to the great lakes, a triumph for engineering in this country.

In addition, Northerners did not show their wealth as much, sometimes keeping it hidden in bank vaults. They were also less willing to settle disputes with a gun than men from the South.

Walter wondered, "Now, why would someone like Jackson be accompanied by someone as impressive as this?" Then Walter recalled learning that Jackson migrated from up North looking for a future in cotton and had been a well-to-do man for some time.

Yes, it was obvious; the elite young lady had the trappings of an aristocrat, and was definitely pleasing to the eye. But was she one of those uppity snobs, like the few Northern visitors he'd encountered in town?

Frankly, he had not been surprised by their condescending attitude towards him, not knowing that he felt as they did about many issues.

Walter continued contemplating the possible attributes of the young beauty as he made his way down the staircase into the entry hall.

"Hello Jackson, and to what do I owe this unexpected pleasure?" Walter tried to sound neighborly, while his eyes looked directly at the mysterious young lady.

Jackson shuffled a bit, clearly uncomfortable with his obvious intrusion.

"Walt, I thought I'd stop in, uh, to see if you could use some help with that fence mending of yours. Thought it would be getting dark soon and you wouldn't finish it today without a bit of help. I felt guilty keeping you so long after Sunday services," Jackson paused hoping for a bit of reassurance from his unsuspecting host.

"How very neighborly of you Jackson," Walter quipped. He was well aware that Mr. Jackson didn't know the first thing about how to repair the fence, and had no intention of doing anything, still dressed in his Sunday best and three women in tow.

"Well, I thought since I'm stopping by, I'd use the trip to bring my daughters out for a bit of late afternoon air. They don't get out as much as they'd like now, since their chaperone had to go 'cause her mother caught ill," Jackson added.

Walter was well aware that if the girls ever had a chaperone or ladies maid who wasn't an unpaid slave, she left because Jackson could not afford to pay for the extra help. However, being a gentleman, he allowed the proud man to maintain his self-respect and went along with the charade.

"I'm sure that was a disappointment," Walter sympathized, and then turned to address himself to the daughters.

"Always happy to have the pleasure of seeing you delightful young ladies twice in the same day," he beamed at them. Both Jean and Marie pretended to be embarrassed, however were delighted at such blatant male attention. Walter smiled, feeling glad only of the appearance of the still unnamed young lady in their midst.

Becoming impatient with their lack of manners, he belatedly added, "But I don't believe I've had the pleasure of meeting this particular young lady to your right, Jackson."

Quickly, Jean, the eldest, spoke before her father could respond. "Oh, this is just our cousin Jacqueline from Maine. She won't be here much longer. She, Uncle Fred, and Aunt Lucille are visiting for a short while."

He noted that Jackson's daughter spoke of her cousin in a dismissive tone that communicated that this addition to her family was of no importance and should be of no interest to their host.

Walter was pleased, however, when the graceful young lady with sage green eyes and hair as dark as molasses, extended her slim, delicate fingers in his direction.

"Hello," she spoke in a soft musical manner. "As my cousin so adeptly put it, my name is Jacqueline... Jacqueline Levenston and I am very pleased to make your acquaintance, sir."

Walter liked the direct approach of this cultured damsel although he didn't appreciate being addressed as "sir," not by her. He wished the rest of the party would depart so he could discover more about this delightful young woman.

Jackson suddenly broke in, "Jacqueline is my sister Lucille's daughter- brought up in the best schools in the east —she was. Well versed in poetry, the arts, and languages, too. She's a lot like my girls; they all play the pianoforte like they were born to it."

Walter could not imagine this charming miss to be anything like the two girls being "presented" to him for the past few hours. It wasn't that they were that homely. They didn't look bad at all: Long straight russet-colored hair, wavy light-brown on the other; nice eyes, a bit of a large nose on one of the daughters, small mouths, and smooth ivory complexions. Not bad at all. So why did everything about them spell d-e-s-p-e-r-a-t-e? If there was one thing Walter never appreciated was someone seeking his attention for all the wrong reasons. Mainly, their father was beginning to rub Walter the wrong way. It was one thing to want to be neighborly; to bring over a baked pie from the wife, or stop to talk as you're riding past. But it was another thing to drop in uninvited on a Sunday afternoon with half the family, under the pretense of offering help where none is needed or truly available. There was a way to get to know someone and to be known by them and this wasn't it, he felt.

Maybe he shouldn't hold his feelings for the father against the girls, he wasn't sure. But one thing he was sure of was that he didn't want Jackson for a father-in-law, and that was certainly what the older man was after. The only reason Walter did not politely turn them all away after a few pleasantries and the offer to get to his fence mended, was because of the appearance of Jacqueline.

"Won't you all please come into the drawing room? If you have not eaten yet, I will ask Ciaok to bring us tea and sandwiches," he offered. Walter knew they could not have had time to eat. They must have dropped off the wife, picked up the niece, and come right over. He had barely changed his Sunday clothes before they appeared at his door.

"That would be wonderful," exclaimed Jacqueline. "I am so very famished. By the way please call me Lena."

"Such a simple-sounding name for one so polished looking?" Walter offered questioningly.

"My family called me Lena when I was young, before entering boarding school. The name has always fit me better than Jacqueline. Actually, I think Lena is quite wonderful, and far less pretentious than Jacqueline."

"There's nothing pretentious about a beautiful lady with a name to match," Walter said.

"Now if you looked like a female version of me and carried yourself unbecomingly with a crude speaking voice besides, and had the name Jacqueline, then perhaps that would be pretentious," he assured her.

Lena couldn't help but laugh, picturing the ridiculous sight of Walter with long dark wavy hair instead of his fair, handsome, strong features.

"You know, on second thought," she teased, "you wouldn't look too bad as a female. You would be quite attractive in most circles, especially in Paris."

"Well then, thank goodness we do not live in Paris," Walter said. "I take it that you have visited there. What did you think of the place?"

"It is more glorious than you could ever imagine. I was there last year for the summer after completing finishing school. The trip was the final touch in the quest to become the total well-rounded young lady of the world," she joked.

"Well you don't sound very appreciative," Walter noted.

"Oh, but I am. I enjoyed it immensely. One thing that people learn about me, and that all the years of boarding and finishing school could not diminish, is my sometimes ill-advised view that life is to be laughed at in order to be enjoyed. My instructors considered this perspective on life a detriment to my education to become the perfect lady," she feigned their displeasure.

As Walter and Lena continued, he realized they had all but forgotten the others in the room. Only Ciaok coming in to serve the tea and sandwiches brought them both back to the reality of the others sitting there with them.

Walter immediately tried to include the other girls in the conversation, but by now they seemed to be quite annoyed at having been ignored for so long by their host, and then finally included as an after-thought.

"Would either of you ladies like to do the honors?" He kindly suggested, hoping that one of the ignored young women would be satisfied playing hostess and serving the late afternoon tea, as custom dictated.

His perfunctory request went unnoticed, as the girls continued to brood over their previous neglect.

Lena took the opportunity to properly smooth over the slowly escalating situation by passing one of the hand embroidered cloths to each of her cousins then carefully pouring the tea into the delicate china cups, offering the first one to Jean, then to her sister.

"Would you like a sandwich uncle?" Lena asked, as she passed an exquisite looking supper platter.

Walter breathed a sigh of relief, grateful for Lena's adroit maneuvering, and then attempted again, himself to get the two injured parties back in good spirits.

"I've heard a lot the last few weeks about this festival of some sort coming up in a few months," he baited, turning to Jean. "Something about everyone in town being involved. I felt a bit the outsider while listening, since it seemed I was the lone soul who knew nothing about this big 'shin-dig'."

"Shindig? No-how," Jean disagreed, rising to the bait. "Why it's only the most high-faluting affair in the entire state and will be for years to come," she embellished.

Walter, happy that his plan had worked, took great pains to look and listen attentively while secretly paying close attention to Lena across the table.

"Oh, maybe we'll get to waltz to the fine chamber and classical music from across the ocean. It will be perfect for all those who want to become enlightened in these parts. Yes, a fine weekend of culture, music, and dancing. It is straight from the upper crust, almost royalty.

Some women will even order their dresses from Paris," Jean spoke to impress.

Walter graciously interrupted, "Don't you think that's going a bit far, for these parts. Don't get me wrong, I understand that you believe this to be the biggest event ever, but a dress made for a queen, well..."

"I didn't say the dresses would be made for the queen," Jean shot back.

Walter had to watch himself not to upset her again.

"Please go on, I didn't mean to interrupt," he begged her pardon.

"I read that the program will consist of quality music concentrating on the 17th an 18th century Rodeau sound," she continued in her attempt to sound proper in a high-pitched voice.

"Rondeau...?" Lena broke in this time.

"Yes Rondeau, my little unenlightened cousin. In my born days, I never would have thought you didn't know music," Jean spoke condescendingly, believing herself to be a cut above her proper boarding school-educated cousin in this area of music appreciation.

"Please explain Rondeau music to us all, "Walter appealed as he tried to bring himself back into his neighbor's good graces.

The eldest daughter rambled on and on about the newer French Baroque instrumental music of the upcoming festival, while her sister added some additional details on the joys of attending a similar gathering the previous year, and Walter hoped—no prayed—for a conclusion to what was becoming a never-ending afternoon visit.

"Well would you look at the time," cut in Jackson, as if answering Walter's prayers. "Walt, if we are going to get to that fence we'd better get started."

Walter knew Jackson had no idea of what to do with the fence. And even if he spent the next two hours giving instructions to the man, the fence would probably look the same as it did at this moment, or worse.

"Jackson, I definitely appreciate your offer, but I'm going to have to decline." Walter spoke up, offering his visitor a way out. "You see, this is a job that requires a man to get down in the dirt and get as filthy as swine and that Sunday suit you still have on, just won't do."

"Well my friend, if you say so," the older man breathed a sigh of relief. "Can't say that I wasn't looking forward to getting at it, though."

"That's quite alright; maybe I can use your help some other time." Walter assured him, while hoping that day would never come.

"Yes, yes some other time for sure," Jackson spoke hurriedly rising to make his way to the entry hall before the other man changed his mind.

Walter offered his hand to each young lady—adding his delight in meeting young Jacqueline who was called Lena.

Before today, the cousin felt sure she had made the wrong decision in coming here with her parents for three weeks. She wondered, "What was there to do?"Her cousins were not exciting, in any way. All they could think or talk about was what they used to have and things they used to do. And all her uncle did, day after day, was plot how to get rid of them. There were many more interesting things she could be doing back home, she'd told herself.

Moving towards the entry hall first, Walter attempted to speak to Lena again quietly without the others hearing. "I hope to see you again before you go back home to Maine. Possibly, you and your parents could join me for dinner one evening before you leave," he proposed.

Walter felt pleased with himself having gotten the chance to speak to the captivating girl alone, without the intrusion of the cousins and uncle. Perhaps, if her parents came with her, even they would be less of a distraction than the Jackson's in their irritating attempt to steer all of Walter's attention towards Jean and the other sister.

Unfortunately for Walter, the elder sister, Jean possessed hearing that extended clear from the drawing room into the front hall. "Do tell, Mr. Neuman, I think we all would be plum delighted to have dinner with you sometime this week. Is that before you come by next Sunday for dinner or after?" she added.

Walter looked down at the floor of the entry hall, feeling somehow furious. He opened his mouth to speak, but nothing came out—thank goodness. Finding his voice, he stammered, "W-Well nothing's definite, uh, I wasn't sure of the date, but as soon as I am, I'll send Ciaok over with an invitation."

Lena, also looking on in disbelief at her cousin's obvious intrusion tried to save everyone embarrassment, by adding, "Yes we'll all look forward to hearing from you then."

As the group stepped out of the entry hall onto the open porch, Walter tensed as Jean stopped short, turned completely around and looked long and hard at his expression and then turned to stare at her cousin Lena walking ahead with the others.

Squinting and scowling, Jean called out, "Daddy", beckoning her father back and latched onto his arm to lead the way to the small coach for the short ride home.

****

Several days later, Walter decided that although he wanted to see Lena again, he could think of no way that he could gracefully get out of including the Jacksons in the invitation. Jean gave him the chills and he had no desire whatsoever, to see her again. So, the best he could do was to have Ciaok take over his deepest regrets that he unfortunately did not have an evening free before Lena and her family departed next week. He wished them the best and a safe trip home. Meanwhile, he thought he'd come up with a gentlemanly way to bow out of next Sunday, too.

Upon the letter's arrival, Lena looked at the message and sighed. She had looked forward to seeing Walter Neuman again, but decided it couldn't be helped. She knew Jean's obvious intrusion and disapproval had everything to do with his suddenly not being able to find an evening free. However, Lena felt he enjoyed her company just as much as she did his and they would find a way to see each other again.

Jean took the news even harder, throwing her hairbrush across the room. It landed on her frumpy well-worn bedcovers. She'd decided that Walter Neuman wasn't going to get out of a promise that easily. His word should have been enough, especially since she ran straight out and spent scarce money on a matching hat from that new shop up in Millville, just for the occasion. It didn't matter that he was expected to dinner next Sunday; he should have kept his word for this visit too. Now, she would have to wait until Sunday to impress him with her delightful new purchase; and impressed she knew he would be.

Years later, Walter would think of that fateful Sunday afternoon and his young "Lena" quite often. He would also wonder when it all began to go wrong.

Chapter Nine

Molly continued to accompany her mother to the Neuman household for the next six weeks. All that was on her mind each day was the money she earned, which brought her one step closer to whirling around the ballroom floor in that fine-looking satin blue gown.   Turning fifteen this past week, Molly had gone into town with ma to pick the material for it.

It would take at least two weeks for her mother to make the long-awaited creation, but that was just enough time. She had the kitchen table all spread out with the homemade pattern of the outfit she felt mature enough to wear in every way. The thought of it made her work with delight around the Neuman house while she dusted and polished. Beside herself, she began to sing with abandon that was until ma stepped in.

"Molly!! For lands sake," her mother cautioned. "It's one thing to sing softly and the right kind of songs, but not that caterwauling.

"Why girl, you sound like of a bunch of squawking hens chasing a rooster out of the henhouse."

"Aw' ma, I can't help it. I'm FIFTEEN... and I'm going to the ball!"Molly screeched even louder.

"Hush girl, hush!" Warned her mother, hoping no one would come to investigate.

****

On Monday evening, Molly walked back home alone, since ma had to stay late to help plan a garden luncheon that Mrs. Neuman was holding for her weekly lady's group gathering. There were times when Molly thought it would have been exciting to stand nearby and listen to all the gossip, but it was obvious that the lady of the house wasn't having that, telling her to "shoo" like some unwanted stray.

Since the sun had not yet gone down, Molly decided not to go straight home, but take the extra-long way around the back of the estate, heading in the direction of the neighboring plantation. She thought how funny old Mr. Jackson, who's lived five miles away ever since she could remember, refers to his property as the "big plantation." While Mr. Neuman who's land is twenty times the size of Mr. Jackson's, doesn't call his place anything in particular. Referring to Mr. Neuman's land as an estate, would have sounded much more refined to Molly's ears, than Mr. Jackson's "big plantation."

She listened to the dogs barking in the distance and thought maybe she should turn around and go home. But then a few barking hounds never scared her before; so why should they now? Molly took her time walking through the shadows and shade-yielding trees, bypassing the dirt paths, continuing on in the direction of the "big plantation.' As she drew closer, Molly noted that the place had indeed gotten even better than when she'd first seen it years ago. Actually, Alex told her that he'd heard that it was "good-looking" years ago, then it got run down, and then it got "right-nice" again. He said it had something to do with the Jackson family losing their help, having no money, and then mysteriously getting loads of money again.

So, from what Molly could gather, the house must have gotten fixed up quite a bit. Why it was even better than when she was here last year. It looked like they added some more rooms. Molly could tell that they had to have the original house repainted, with new windows and doors just so it wouldn't look out of place with the new part. They even had a side path put out back to connect their property with the main road. Probably, she thought, so they wouldn't have so much trouble driving that new coach she'd seen them riding in to town last year.

As Molly passed four hardy pecan trees at the edge of the property, in the distance she could see someone sitting outside on the wide porch that extended all the way around the newly improved house.

From what she could make out, it was a body she had never seen before—not from around here. Molly knew there were three daughters who grew up in the old house long before; first when it was so grand and even when it became run down. But the daughters either married or left and hadn't been back since, except for their mother's funeral years ago.

Small twigs crackled under Molly's feet as she approached the front of the house. The woman turned around in the direction of the faint echoing sound and looked directly into the curious eyes of the oncoming uninvited visitor.

"Yes, may I help you?" The owl-eyed, spinsterish, not-so-old woman cackled with a dry tone and raised eyebrow. Her face showed contempt for this brazen young thing whose youth magnified her own matronly status.

"No help needed" Molly smiled nonchalantly, "I'm just out for a bit of fresh evening air."

"Well it looks as if you strayed a bit too far. I'm sure the evening air is the same where you came from as it is on my estate," the woman reprimanded her.

Molly thought, there they go again with that business. Now it's an estate, not a "big plantation." Maybe they figured they'd moved up a bit, she almost laughed aloud, but quickly stopped herself.

Not intimidated by the surly woman's ways, Molly purposely pressed on.

"You live here?"Molly asked.

The woman grumbled, then gave a dismissive nod.

"Well... I had no idea," Molly shot back, "I've come near here from time to time for going on seven years and I've never seen the likes of you cavorting on the BIG PLANTATION before." .

"First of all, it's not called that anymore and I don't cavort, as you put it. But more so, I don't know who you are, or what you are doing here, so I don't owe the likes of you any explanation! Therefore, go immediately you little upstart!" She shouted haughtily.

Molly stood her ground. She was not used to being dismissed in such a manner... at least not around here.

"Who are you anyway, lady?" You don't have to have a conniption fit and yell at me like a jackal," Molly retorted fearlessly.

Completely taken aback by this feisty girl's impertinence, the outraged adversary stood up.

"Why... why you little low-life heathen!" She screamed for all within earshot to hear.

The shouting reached the ears of old Mr. Jackson who crept out unto his porch. He was getting around on a walking stick these days. The soft, rhythmic thud of the cane soundly kept pace with his steps as he moved delicately, carried by unsteady feet. His curved spine and white hair spoke of a man nearing seventy years.

Jackson walked into the tense altercation between the two and looked out to see Molly backing away in the direction of the large pecan tree. He spoke up in a short raspy whisper, "Jean, stop being so ornery, and leave the girl alone. She's always prattling on, but she's of no account. She's the young one of the longtime woman on Walter and Lena's place. You remember?"

At the mention of her cousin Lena and Walter Neuman, Jean became fiercer than ever, remembering that afternoon almost twenty years ago when that scoundrel reneged on both dinner engagements and distanced himself from her family. Jean hadn't realized, at the time, that he continued to keep company with her cousin by letter and that they would soon marry. She had struggled long and hard to get past it, even going as far as to move back up North and re-invent herself.

Interrupting the elderly man, she insisted, "No father, I remember nothing. As far as I'm concerned here is just a despicable little trespasser, whom I have already told to leave."

Jackson was much too tired for another battle with his peevish daughter. She seemed to be older than her thirty-nine years. So much so that a few months with her in the house felt like years. He'd hoped her time up North would make her more gentle and easygoing; instead she was worse than ever. He thought he probably should say something to her, but always felt a bit guilty; thinking it could be his and the missus' fault — God rest her soul— that Jean turned out the way she did.

He decided instead to caution the girl: "Well, little Miss Molly, I recollect that's what your name is, I think you better get on home now. It's almost sun set. I'm sure your mama will be looking for you to help her with something," he said, almost apologetically.

Molly tried to calmly take in what was being said to her. It wouldn't have been so bad if old Mr. Jackson had asked her to "run along." When she was younger, she had sometimes come over and talked his ears off. Since he had no one else to talk to then, he was a willing listener, most of the time. Whenever he'd had enough of the young girl's constant chatter, he'd tell her to "get on home, you little chatterbox." Until now, Molly always wondered if he knew her proper name.

But this cantankerous fang-fighting Jean-person was one that Molly wasn't going to take to at all.

"I hope she goes back wherever she's been for the past ten years. Mean, moldy old crone!" Molly muttered just loud enough to be heard by both Jacksons before rustling away, crunching pecan castoffs underfoot, into the near dusk.

Chapter Ten

With the afternoon sun going down, Molly headed towards her favorite place hoping to wash away the remnants of this unexpectedly humiliating experience.

Molly knew maybe she was always a bit sheltered around here, but this was home. She could be herself here, if nowhere else. Molly also knew how to put on an act when she ventured into town. Why not here? 'Cause this was not town or anywhere near it, she told herself.

Molly paced along the edge of the lake-like pond envisioning what might be in-store for her. Scores of tiny little flowers, duckweeds, she'd remembered Jake calling them, floated atop of the water, opening where she paused and touched her right heel. Blossoming for the first and only time that season, hundreds of thousands of the miniature white flowers crowded close together, a cottony blanket hugging and warming the scenic pond's cool blue shore line.

Molly wondered would it be a shock to her little lake when that soft fluffy covering rolled away in a few weeks.

Looking around, she recalled how she marveled anew the first time she visited here with Alex:

With a life of its own, the lake approached as we strolled through the avenue of trees, swiveling on our heels to transfix our eyes to the full glorious sight. The tranquil waters held on to various shades of blue, echoing the early morning sky. Near the edge, the color was a light shade, almost celestial; as it moved inward it changed from celestial to nearly violet. Willows and spruces on the other end of the pond were visible on the water's surface. Their leaves rustling in alternating colors, as soft waves undulated, swaying to a song of their own.

Over the years, the young girl had become accustomed to a different way of life than most. She wasn't at all sure how to put it into words.   In her surroundings, within a five-mile radius, she could be inspiring, outspoken, and imaginative. While outside "her world," in what ma and others call "the real world," she felt obliged to put on a show.

For the second time, she felt hope slipping away from her. The first humiliation she never talked about and buried far down within her. Molly didn't want to react now that this encounter today had again infringed on "her world."

Feeling dejected, she turned and reluctantly glanced back toward the Jackson "estate" in the near distance. Molly decided then and there she had no choice but to move on and forget everything that had just happened. Like that tiny flower, it will soon sink to the bottom of the water column and emerge again next time, brand new.

Renewed faith sparked Molly's limbs; her legs lunged forward in a bolting rush to get home before nightfall. Darkness had set in when Molly met her mother going into the house.

She knew not to burden ma with the embarrassment she had just suffered. Her mother had enough to think about and she didn't need any more trouble, Molly concluded.

As Molly strode towards her, Enola looked at her daughter's blank, faraway stare and wondered what was behind it. She didn't have the heart to tell her just yet what had been discussed between Jake and her. But Enola knew she would have to, very soon.

****

There were only two short weeks left to prepare for the upcoming Autumn Festival. Molly didn't know what to do next. She felt like she might have gotten herself into more than she could handle in designing her own ball costume. It took eons to get it sketched and cut out exactly to her liking, such that she was sure her mother would not have enough time to put it together to her specifications. Ma was able to get some of the material from Ms. Neuman's pristinely kept castoffs and the rest on a recent visit to ole' Mr. Richmond's store, disguised as a purchase for Mrs. Neman. Molly got the idea for the gown by peeking at Mrs. Neuman's *Godley Lady's Book*, while dusting the things on her night table.

The design was to be a Princess Polonaise dress in deep sea blue with a fitted, yet voluminous overskirt attached to the bodice and draped up just a bit at the rump. Molly could leave it unbuttoned from the waist down to reveal her pretty underskirt in pale ivory. She wanted it to be a masterpiece, a dress that no one could take their eyes off, no matter how hard they tried.

That evening, as Molly and her mother worked together on the elegant gown, ma reminisced about the first time folks who were "non-landowners," as they put it, were allowed to attend the festival. "There were only about thirty or thirty-five of us from around town who were allowed that privilege," Enola recalled. "I was never sure what the measure was that had to be met in order to be one of those invited to come.

The only thing I heard tell was that; the ones—
the non-landowners we were called— who were
there; we were talked about town to be some of
the finest-looking people who attended the festival."

Jake walked in on the middle of the story, after finishing up outside. He listened a bit then
added his own male perspective. He had finally
attended the last two times it was held and gave a
glowing description of one young lady in particular at the last event. He described a stunning, exotic, looking girl whose beauty had smitten him
and most of the other men there.

"Sounds a lot like me, huh?" Molly quipped.

Jake responded teasingly, "Not at all my dear
sister. Not one bit."

"I really did like that girl though," he added, as
his mother moved into the back room.
"...thought about asking to court her.

"I had all these poems I'd saved up from when
I was in Mr. Temple's class years earlier. I was
pretty good too. Still write some from time to
time. I thought I could try to write some songs to
sing to her, if she agreed to allow me to come see
her. I wonder whatever happened to her."

He paused, waiting for some kind of a response. Spying his sister's total disinterest in anything he was saying, he let the subject go.

Molly was quite sure, beyond any doubt, that
she would soon burst with anticipation. How
much longer could she be expected to stand the
wait? She wondered.

Every waking moment, envisioning an exciting and wondrous new adventure that included seeing herself just as exquisite, just as alluring, and even more exciting than that "belle of the ball" her brother thought she hadn't heard enough about.

Molly was walking on air and nothing, absolutely nothing, could dull her spirits, not even any humiliating experiences, and certainly not that long ago talk about moving.

Ma came back into the front room holding the bottom half of Molly's blue "little piece of heaven" gown in her arms. She handed Molly the needle to re-thread, since her own close-up vision wasn't what it used to be. She needed to measure Molly around the waist to have the dress fit and drape right. Jake with his numbers sense, made up a tape of numbers on a line on a long cut strip of leftover cotton material. Molly marveled at how precisely spaced the numbers and lines were. Ma was able to wrap the cloth around her top, middle and bottom.

Jake pointed out, "See how the beginning and the end can come together on the strip, even with all the numbers that pass in between them, they still meet at the same spot. There's really no beginning and no end. Just keeps going round and round. The only stopping points are those little lines above the numbers and in between them, the ones in between are parts of the whole or the fractions.

"I'm no idiot Jake," Molly protested, "I know my fractions."

"That's not what I mean girl... listen," he demanded.

"I surely have no time for this." She objected.

"No Molly... ma, this thing, this here line goes on without ending. The only time it stops is for special points so we can measure, then it continues on again. Like we stop, ponder and take stock of our life for awhile when a baby's born, on our birthdays, graduations, memorable times, like wedding days, when someone dies, and then we move on.

There he goes mixing his numbers sense with that poetry stuff.

Molly sighed.

"Okay Jake, Whatever you say." I shouldn't have ignored him earlier, she thought, look what I ended up with.

Hoping her mother felt the same, Molly caught her looking down at the hem of Molly's ball gown, needle in her hand, with a strange wistful looking expression. Feeling she was being watched, ma quickly looked up from Jake to Molly forcing a half-smile to the corner of face, bringing her daughter's thoughts back to her own troubles. But Molly reminded herself of her vow.

"Nothing at all will distract me from my course, so be it!" She proclaimed aloud.

Chapter Eleven

Feeling as if she had challenged the fates with her declaration—something she didn't even believe in— Molly learned her mother was bringing up the subject of moving once more. Jake had confided to Molly that just last week ma discussed it with him again. He said that all the wonderful talk about the Autumn Festivals ma had attended in the past was a cover for what was really bothering her. Jake said she had opened up to him when she followed him out front to bring in water for the evening wash before Molly got home.

He revealed that ma told him that she had no intention of bringing up the notion again, but that she had no other choice.

"Jake, how do you like living here and working at the mill for Mr. Neuman," she began.

Not being one to stir up trouble, he carefully kept his answer brief, "I like it just fine, ma."

"Okay, but can you tell me a little more?" His mother asked.

"What more do you want to know, ma?" Jake questioned.

"What do you like about what you do, boy?" Her voice rose sharply, losing patience with her son's lack of response.

Noticing her son's surprised expression, Enola apologized.

"I'm sorry. I shouldn't shout or say 'boy' either," she continued more calmly. "I know you are not a boy, not anymore. You're a man. And your sister is a young lady. You both grew up before I knew what was happening. I always thought about what kind of young man you'd grow up to be, as I watched you, swimming in the lake with Mr. Neuman's children in the summers. I'd watch you and hope that you and your sister would have a better life than I had."

"Ma, I never knew you were watching us then," Jake placed his hand on his mother's rounded shoulder.

"I guess maybe 'cause you and me never talked much about those kinds of things," he continued, "You always seemed to be trying to keep us walking a straight path. You know, help-ing us, especially Molly, keep out of trouble."

"Of course I didn't want you children to see my worries. It was more important for you to know that you were loved and you knew how to survive in this here world. It was my job to teach you, and I was determined to make sure that you learned well," Enola revealed.

Jake frowned remembering his original con-cern over his mother's strange mood, "Ma, is eve-rything okay? I mean you're not sick or any-thing?"

"Sick?" Enola ran her hands through her dark, slightly graying hair. "No, not this time, don't sound so worried son.

"I'll have you know, I've been sicker than you'll ever realize, many times over the years. But with the help of the good Lord, I've always been able to bounce back before you children or the Neuman's knew how really bad off I was. But no," she repeated, "I'm not sick now."

"That's a relief, ma, because I've seen you looking really worried about something these last few months. I didn't know if I should say any-thing about it or not."

"I have had something on my mind, Jake. You weren't wrong. It's something that I've mentioned a time or two with both you and your sister," Enola reminded him, picking up the heavy bucket then putting it back down again.

"You don't mean that moving-on business, do you, ma?" Jake questioned, taking the distracting pail from her.

"Yes, I do." Enola responded, nodding slowly, leading the way back towards the shanty.

"But ma, I thought you gave up that idea, since we didn't hear anymore about it again." Jake followed, looking worried again.

"No I never gave it up. But I did see how it upset you, and especially Molly. So I thought I wouldn't bring it up again unless I really had to."

"Well, do you?" Jake questioned, with a frown.

"What?" Enola asked, her troubled mind easily slipping far away for that moment.

"Do you really have to bring it up again, ma?" Jake demanded, looking puzzled at his mother's clear lack of focus. He was now losing patience himself.

"Yes, I do dear," Enola said again apologetically.

"Why?" Jake was asking all the questions now.

"I never wanted to tell you this because you considered Mr. and Mrs. Neuman and their children like family, but I think you surely have to know now."

"What, mom? Come on, you're scaring me!"
"What is it?"

"They want me to leave!" Enola suddenly blurted out.

"What, who wants you to leave, ma? You don't mean the Neumans?" Jake stared at her in disbelief.

"They want me to leave Jake, and you and Molly to go with me," she added.

"But I don't understand! You haven't told Molly yet, have you? Does she know anything about this? And where will we go?" Jake's voice shook, unleashing a string of questions.

"No, you being the oldest, and the man of the family," Enola revealed— responding to only one of his questions, "I wanted to tell you first."

Jake turned around and paced back and forth from the water pump to the door of the well-built little shanty. This was the only home he could remember. It was his responsibility, he felt, to determine exactly what this would mean for his mother, sister, and him.

"Okay, ma, you say they want us to go, but you haven't said why or where," Jake noted, searching for answers.

"Jake, it's their land, always has been. We never really owned it. They don't have to give us a reason or anything else for that matter," his mother reminded him.

"Yeah, ok, ma, but it never was like that with us. I know, because you told me a long time ago, that this place was yours. They never acted like it was their house, ever. They never showed us anything but kindness and a respect of some sort. They're good to everyone, all the sharecroppers on the land, and just as good to us. Darn it, ma,

we've been here longer than anybody, even before the war, you were here."

Moving inside, Enola looked down at the
brown plank flooring— she'd always felt fortunate to have— before responding truthfully,
"From what I understand, they need this house
because it is the largest of the shanties. Mrs.
Neuman wants her aunt to come and live near
them since her aunt's husband died. Her aunt
has always has been proud and won't want to live
free in the main house like a charity case. Mrs.
Neuman offered to redo this place for her aunt
and she has accepted. So it's all set and there's
nothing we can do."

"So you mean everything is all set and we are
being forced out? Jake concluded, disbelievingly,
"When?"

"Come spring. That's when Mrs. Neuman
thinks her aunt will be ready to make the trip
with all of her belongings. I'm told she's been
grieving something fierce over her husband and
needs time to get her things in order before she
can take a final trip from up North."

"Up North? You mean she wants to come here
after living up North all her life?

"What part?" He asked, obviously weary now,
bending to sit down at the kitchen table.

"Maine or Boston, I think most of Mrs.
Neuman's people are from around there." Enola
remembered, joining her son at the table.

"Is the aunt part of that group visiting up at the house this week?" Jake continued questioning.

"Yes, well, she's the aunt to several of them, if that's what you mean." Enola offered.

"I can understand folks visiting, but how can somebody from up there want to come live here, especially at her age. I bet she's about 80 or something isn't she?"

Enola chuckled in spite of her dilemma. "No, she's closer to 60, maybe late 50s, and she's the aunt who's been traveling all over the world with her husband— so she can live just about anywhere."

Enola watched her son closely. He looked so much older, just in these last few moments. She didn't want to cast this burden on her children, but it couldn't be helped.

"I just thought you should know, son. You are grown enough now to make plans of your own. I 'd like to have you with me always, but I know that can't be," his mother bemoaned— attempting a smile hoping to boost both their spirits. However, she couldn't contain that far away look her son and daughter have come to understand.

Jake tried to smile back—- for his mother's sake.

Now anxious about his immediate future, he stammered, "Ma--Mother, I guess I better get as much practice as I can, using that proper English you been pushing on me and Molly for years."

Obviously, in an effort to steady himself again, he focused on his sister's reaction to the news.

Gently touching his mother's arm, Jake spoke quietly, "I would like to tell Molly. I know how hard it is for you, and I don't want her blaming you for anything. I want it to come from me. She and I can help each other get through this."

"Thank you, dear. Don't tell her yet, though. Just wait until after the festival to break the news. She's so out of control now, I'd hate to bring this sorrowful hurt on her. Let her have her moment," Enola sighed.

"Oh, I won't break the whole story to her yet," Jake promised his mother, "maybe bits and pieces, just enough so she won't be completely destroyed when time finally comes to tell her everything."

****

Genuinely apprehensive, as promised, Jake left out quite a few details when relaying the dialogue between he and his mother to his sister. All Molly knew was that they just may have to move; but not where or why. Jake figured he had plenty of time to tell her the entire dilemma in the weeks ahead. "Let Molly be Molly for as long as she can," he had agreed, as newly self-appointed leader of his family.

The young girl's spirits were still pretty high, even with the news. For her, it was not all that new—this idea of possibly moving. Ma had mentioned it before.

It's just that Molly thought that was all done with—for good. Since ma didn't seem too concerned about the situation, Molly figured she wasn't going to make a big deal out of it, either. Anyway the biggest weekend of her life was coming up and she would not, no matter what, have it spoiled by anything. And definitely not by something that may not happen anyway. Isn't that what Jake said? She convinced herself.

Chapter Twelve

It's been said that some people never learn. Molly didn't "reckon" on being one of those people, not any more. For this reason, she took great pains working up at the Neuman house to develop a comfortable routine. Each day, since the first few weeks, she followed the schedule set out before her and never deviated from it.

However, her determination to stay focused— her mapped out plan— was notably thwarted that particular afternoon—the one she tried her almighty best to forget.

As Molly recalled, the time was early last month, just two and a half weeks after she started helping her mother up at the estate. That's when the unreal "confrontation" occurred. From it, she would try to learn, and then maybe she really could forget for always. She had to.

When it happened, Molly was sitting down polishing all the radiant shiny silver Mrs. Neuman prides herself on.

Mrs. Neuman's relatives, visiting from up North, had arrived the night before. Molly had never seen this group before. Even though she understood that they had met most of the household staff when they arrived, she hadn't seen them. This was her way of trying to explain, even to herself, why what happened had happened.

Molly was sitting in the dining room corner with a silver ladle and polish rag in hand, when she was startled by someone shouting, "You, girl!"

At the time, she had no idea that the agitated shrill voice was directed at her. "GIRL!!" the voice croaked again, even much louder and harsher this time, "I'M TALKING TO YOU!"

Molly turned and was stunned to see a tall muscular gentleman with piercing blue eyes and a scowl to match. He was dressed in dark gray trousers, a white shirt and tie. "Are you addressing me, sir?" She questioned, placing her hand on her breast in both acknowledgment and disbelief.

"You know damned well who I'm talking to… How d-dare you ignore me!" He stammered, taking note of Molly's physical beauty, but obviously unfazed by it. She clearly didn't know her place, he believed.

"Sir," she met his stare directly, "I do not make a habit of ignoring people, not anyone...even you. If I were under the impression that you were speaking to me, even in such a shrill, unkind voice, I would have acknowledged you, in one way or another. I assure you."

Molly quickly realized she had made a grave error in her attempt to size up and take down this opponent. Feeling the ire rise up in her, she'd tried to catch it, but she couldn't. Although what she saw next made her absolutely certain of her mistake.

She actually thought she saw steam coming out of the man's trembling nostrils, while drops of sweat beaded on his forehead. His face now looked like a turnip sprinkled with purple blotches all over.

In spite of herself, Molly continued relentlessly, "And, sir, my name is Molly Elizabeth, not girl. Everyone around here knows that. I have yet to answer to girl, and I'm not going to start now."

Molly knew she was skating on thin ice, but she couldn't control herself, and he had it coming to him. "So you see, sir, I had no way of knowing that you were attempting to get my attention in a manner as uncouth as the one YOU displayed."

With that final pronouncement, the man, bloated almost twice his initial size, seemed to have stopped breathing.

Molly had been determined to stand her ground. No one in the Neuman household had ever treated her so roughly, and she knew no other way to respond to such treatment "at home." She had always felt that way here at the estate, in spite of Mrs. Neuman's strange ways.

Actually, this stranger was the outsider, not me, Molly attempted to reassure herself. He was in "her world." When she thought about it the strange man did look pretty funny, standing there with his hair on end and all red and blue; purple-faced. She swore she could see white horns rising through his copper-colored hair as it rose even higher. She laughed to herself, or so she thought to herself, when she realized he was lunging towards her.

Molly ducked swiftly, so that strands of her wavy chestnut hair twisted around several of the silver utensils she'd been polishing. He grabbed at her hair, which seemed to be wrapped around a particularly long fork. Molly wasn't sure and didn't care. Without further thought, she ran stumbling up the stairs, trying to pry loose the dangling fork. It was caught and hanging from her hair. Screaming for her mother, she prayed harder than she had in her entire life.

Molly rushed to the first open door at the top of the staircase, as the "crazed maniac" was right on her heels. Instantly, she slammed the door in his face and securely locked it from the inside, leaving him pounding on it with murder in his eye.

Mrs. Neuman was in the drawing room writing letters and planning her day when she heard Molly's screams and rushed out, down the long hall, and towards the commotion.

Completely disheveled, the young man stormed back down the long staircase he'd just ascended, as his cousin approached.

"Jason, what in heaven's name is all the noise," she asked.

"That damned wench," he pronounced loud enough through clenched teeth to be heard by Molly upstairs. She carefully cracked the door and slowly emerged from the sanctuary of the room. The utensil now loosened and hidden under the bed.

"To whom are you referring," Lena Neuman asked her second cousin-once removed.

"I don't know who she is," he sputtered, while trying to settle himself. "How in the name of what is decent can you have a girl like that in your house?"

As Molly listened, her anger began to flare up again, surpassing any momentary fear.

"I still don't know to what girl you are referring, but judging from your state and disturbing appearance, I'm almost positive you've encountered Molly," Mrs. Neuman nodded knowingly in the direction of the stairway.

"She's harmless," Mrs. Neuman continued. She simply dismissed Molly with a flip of her hand. "You must try to bear with her, dear cousin.

"I'll admit, she's never known her place. I don't like her behavior anymore than you, but I try to ignore her whenever possible. That usually works best. You must do the same."

"Maybe you don't care about defiance, dear cousin, but I won't stand for it," he stated authoritatively.

"I'm surprised at you Jason, a Bostonian born and bred, acting like a truly insulted Southerner. Yes, I'm shocked," she pretended by opening her mouth and placing both hands over it to display a ladylike show of alarm.

"You've always known I can be a Southerner at heart. Just like you, our parents, and other relatives before us, except Aunt Minnie, of course," he countered.

"Speaking of Aunt Minnie," she changed course; "I've asked her to come and stay with us for a while."

"You're asking for trouble there. But that's your problem, mine is that-that..." he sputtered.

"I don't think I can stay here in this house another day knowing 'that girl' will be around the next corner I turn. I will not trust myself not to take a murderous hand to her if I catch up to her next time."

"You do and you will be marched out of the door, never to return, dear cousin," she assured him. "And I do so like your visits every so often. It's not that I would at all mind giving her the back of my hand every now and then, but...."

Listening to them the whole time, Molly cringed. But now she couldn't stand to hear another word. In a flash, she rushed down the winding staircase, through the entry hall and bolted out of the white double doors. She didn't care whether she was paid for the day or not—it didn't matter. The reason she was working here was the last thing on her mind right now.

She felt such a fool. Even now, after all the warnings, how could she still be shocked by what she heard?

It was just like ma and Jake said, Molly told herself as tears of disillusionment and lost hope streamed down her face.

Utterly crushed, she ran blindly, stumbling as her left foot became heavy with the old ailment. Still, she managed to run away as far as she could from life; the life they wanted for her.

Chapter Thirteen

Molly remembered waking the next morning with swollen eyes and a horrible pounding in her head. She was glad Jake was at the mill pouring over those "books", as he called the rows, columns and pages of numbers he was so good at adding, subtracting, multiplying, and dividing. If he was home he would be asking her questions, telling her how terrible she looked and keeping at her, trying to find out what's wrong. She didn't want him or anyone else to be privy to her frightful, humiliating experience, whether they were there to see it or not. Plus she was afraid for Jake, if he knew what that "demon" said and did to her, he might try to challenge him to a duel or something of the sort. She knew things were different on the Neuman place, but not so different that her brother could challenge a white man. She had planned to tell her mother— who had been outside in the Neuman garden that day when the "ruckus" happened— that she wasn't feeling well and couldn't work the next day.

"I'll work around here today, mother, if that is agreeable to you?" Molly whispered with unusual care, after having placed a cold cloth on her puffy eyes before approaching her mother.

Enola knew when her daughter wasn't well, but she'd felt there was something else behind her sudden change of spirit.

"Dear, I won't ask you the real reason you don't want to go today, but it must be a very good one, since you won't get paid when you don't show up to work," she'd reminded Molly.

"I know," Molly bemoaned, "It can't be helped."

Enola had known not to push the issue further. She only hoped —at the time—that Molly would soon get over whatever was bothering her and back to her usual exasperating, but joyful self.

****

That next day and two days thereafter, Molly's mysterious sudden illness kept her from working at the Neuman house.

At the end of that week, Molly learned that Mrs. Neuman had asked that she not show up for the past week, anyway.

"Not to worry, she will still get her pay," Mrs. Neuman had promised her mother.

When told of this mixed blessing, Molly was helping prepare supper at home.

I knew she didn't like me, Molly thought, but I never knew how much.

Almost losing her grip on her feelings, Molly dashed out the door before finishing supper.

She spent a moment collecting her thoughts, not sure why the "intense dislike" bothered her so— Molly hardened herself to go back in and finish setting the table. A good thing too... remembering she'd forgotten to put the potatoes on to boil; she swung the door open and dashed in.

She found her mother removing the pot from the stove, "Oh ma, you've already finished. I'm so sorry, I forgot the potatoes."

"I've got so much on my mind. I know way too much, you'd say, right?" Molly offered, attempting to play devil's advocate.

"No, don't put words in my mouth, girl. Did you hear me say that?" Enola reprimanded.

"No, but..." Molly began.

"But nothing, missy. You've got to stop this thinking that you know what everyone else is thinking even before they know it!"

"I don't do that. Do I? Well, maybe I do. But that's only because I do know what folks are thinking. That is, I can see it. It comes from years of watching people very closely. And I'm right, most of the time, too!" Molly reassured herself.

"I give up," Enola raised her arms in surrender.

Despite her earlier misery, Molly heartily laughed at her mother's display of theatrics. She continued laughing with almost hysterical abandon as she finished setting the table for supper.

Strangely, she recalled, that disheartening week— almost four weeks ago. It ended with mother helping daughter recapture a spirited lightheartedness. Both strolling arm in arm, out after supper. They went down towards Molly's self-proclaimed paradise humming ma's favorite tune.

"Down by the riverside... down by the riverside... down by the riverside..."

Chapter Fourteen

It was now approaching late October. The air outside suddenly turned unusually warm the day before, so Molly didn't require her worn overcoat to go out. She had hoped that she and her mother would be on their way to town to complete their preparation for the weekend of Molly's dreams. She had come to terms with what had happened to her at the Neuman house last month. She reminded herself that so much had occurred since then and that she was still Molly— a girl whose hopeful existence rested on a countenance which required some memories to be put away forever.

This was the week before the event. As her mother was putting the finishing touches on the dress that Molly was sure would change her life, she searched near her bed and pulled out the only pair of shoes she might be able to wear with her gown.

Everyone must know these old shoes well...she thought. Reserved for Sundays and special days, they were very worn and tight. Molly now realized just how worn they were. There was no question about it; there was no way that she could wear these scuffed up white spool heeled pumps with her "dress from heaven." She turned the shoes over and noticed that the low heel was run down on the outside of each shoe, causing her to lean to the left and to the right. Each step she took looked like an exaggerated swagger.

"Why this could never be the walk of a young lady with proper training," Molly said out loud.

She thought maybe if she could put it to her mother in this way, she might agree to a much-needed new pair. Molly had always took great pride in her powers of persuasion, although she felt on shaky ground lately. Actually, she shuddered to think of her mother's reaction, after the new dress and everything. But she had to give it a try now, since she didn't have much time.

Molly strode into the front room. "Ma-Mother, dear...How are you feeling?" Molly cautiously walked over to where her mother was putting the finishing touches on her satin, sea blue and ivory gown.

"Dear mother, you have no idea how much I love and appreciate you for making this vision of a gown for me." Molly continued, "Just look at it! I don't have to tell you how much I adore it…and *you*—always. How delightful of you to agree to make it for me! I'm absolutely sure there is not a better mother in all of this entire state than my very own," she added with perfect diction.

Enola knew her daughter better than anyone. When Molly went into her display of all things proper; talking, walking, mannerisms, and charm, her mother knew what was coming next. This time it must be an overpowering request, because Molly was putting her all into it.

This mother couldn't help but smile at the dazzling sight her daughter made. Her slim, but shapely, delicate figure was long-limbed and graceful. Her honey-kissed complexion and naturally wavy dark chestnut hair both shone as the midday sunlight came through the small window. Oh, how she wanted so much for this naive, yet lovingly headstrong child!

"Molly, what is it this time?" Enola erased her smiling thoughts, and managed to sound stern.

"Oh ma, you know me too well. Am I so obvious? It's how I really feel, you know. I wasn't acting. That was the real me. At least the way I always think of myself. All your wonderful training is just helping me show everyone the person I see in the looking-glass. Now, tell me, do I seem so very unnatural as my real self, I mean?"

Molly was on the verge of wearing out Enola with some of her convoluted ways. But she had some idea of what was on the girl's heart and mind.

"No dear. You are my divine, intelligent, sweet child, who is going to be the most captivating sight for all to see. "Now, what do you want?" Enola asked, getting back to the point.

"You see, this dress is so-o-o-o very exquisite that its beauty could be completely destroyed with the wrong things," Molly said, slowly pleading her case. "Let's take my shoes, for instance. I don't know if you have noticed, but if you walk behind me on Sunday on the way to church, you will see that I waddle just like a duck in them. And they are turning colors; the heel is way too low and they are no longer white. They're more like a dull yellow, with deep streaks that I can't cover up. So, I was just hoping that... might I please get a pair of those perfectly lovely new-fangled pumps to go with the dress? I saw them in Godey's Lady's Book and they are the newest thing up North with all the ladies of distinction."

"Where will the money come from?" Enola asked.

Molly shot back an answer. "That's the least of my worries. I've saved enough money from helping out at the Neuman's everyday to afford the price of the shoes. All we need to do now is go to one of the stores in town where they can get

them in less than a week; that's all," Molly concluded.

"What do you think it's going to look like to
those townspeople when I take you up there all
high and mighty to get a pair of shoes made like
a lady of distinction from up North?" Her mother
questioned.

"Ma, I don't care what they think up in that
backwater town. I never have, not really," she declared. "They think they know what is proper for
me and what isn't. I have my way of making
those folks think that anything I say or do is
okay."

"She's just that silly little Neuman farm-girl,"
they say to each other and shake their heads.

"Plus," she added, "You know, I know how to
play-act in town."

"And even if they don't like it, they won't say a
word. That's what Jake said. They know better
than to mess with us."

Enola was sure Molly had no idea what Jake
meant, and she had no more time for this kind of
talk. There were things that needed to be done to
just get to the end of this day.

"We'll see, missy. I think it might be okay,"
Enola told her daughter. "We can't go today,
but let me see if we can get the coach for day after tomorrow. It's supposed to rain later in the
week, so if we can't get the carriage, I 'dunno. I
draw the line at showing up to town wet and
muddy."

With her mother warily on board, Molly squealed with delight. "Thank you, ma. My mother! You have no idea how I feel right now. I do love you," she declared.

"Oh, I can imagine. More importantly, I hope you learn how to walk in those things before the festival." Enola laughed, as Molly practically flew out of the door, forgetting all the chores she had to finish. She mumbled something about gathering enough pecans for an arithmetic lesson she was giving at the lake tomorrow.

Enola stood still, watching from the window at her unbridled woman-child. Molly was happy now, but as a mother, Enola was leery of what the future held for her. She hadn't the heart to call her back in to finish her chores.

Her mother walked away from the window and sat back down; worried that Molly still may not have enough money for the shoes. She really had nothing to help her child out. When Molly first approached her with the request for dress shoes, Enola felt sure it would be an impossible one to meet.

Still, Enola hated confronting the reality of hard times. For this reason, she stopped herself from wandering down that "dark dusty road," as she remembered it.

Enola decided she'd "best worry less and work more." After getting up to remove the pot of navy beans from the fire, she moved to the cutting board to peel and cut up potatoes for supper.

With her favorite dull knife, she began by slowly peeling the white potatoes in the basket. She always used it for just this particular chore. Last week when Enola used the sharper one, she was surprised at how badly she'd cut her hand. She didn't need any more problems these days.

Getting up again and passing the window opening, Enola marveled at the sight of her Molly, basket in hand, bending for nuts while still dancing a jig far down the narrow twisting path ahead.

****

Enola didn't know how to tell her daughter what had come about that evening after Jake got home.

Her boy was leaving. Jake had decided in an "all-fired" hurry to go up North and prepare a way for their move— come spring. He said that since he'd just turned 20, he could find a job and get a place for them. It didn't seem to matter how much she cautioned her son on the dangers of going North by himself now, Jake said he was going to be a man and do the right thing by his family. He planned to say his goodbyes tonight when he got in from the mill, then leave come sun up.

Enola felt her daughter had come to depend on her brother more than he, or even she knew. Molly would be devastated.

Chapter Fifteen

Autumn was on full display. Oak and maple trees were already at close to half of their peak fall color, with varying shades of red and gold vying for attention.

"Glad that warm air only lasted for a couple of days. We're gone right back to some cool refreshing times," Enola proclaimed while coming in with the evening water. She was trying to keep the topic light hearted.

Molly had gathered everything she needed for her "class" the next day. She was in her own world now, and completely ignoring her mother's comments.

"I can see it all," she said.

"In just about a week, no one in these parts will be able to say they do not know Molly Elizabeth McCray.

'Why, wasn't that Miss Molly we saw in Mr. Richmond's store the other day," they'll say.

"In spite of themselves," Molly said, "they'll have to admit, that I am beautiful, clever and such a wonderful dancer."

Mimicking everyone's reaction, Molly twirls herself round and round, and not much to her mother's surprise, she trips over a pail filled with water. Soaking wet, she never stops moving— right past the gray picket fence outside the garden at the end of the short lane she continues to practice.

"One Step, T-two…S-step," she slowly loses steam and leisurely ambles through a natural progression of trees lining a shady, dark, cool lane.

Molly begins again, "One Step, Two Step, Back- Back Dip, Side- Side, Dip," as she emerges from the passageway lined with spruce trees. The way opens to "her" rippling lake-like pond about fifty paces ahead.

Here— Molly once shared with ma— the sweet-scented air smells fresher, the juicy persimmons ripen sweeter, the majestic magnolias grow taller, and the whitetail deer roam freer.

"One Step, Two Step…," she pressed on, until the late evening sunlight glistened on her "little lake." Molly had now reached the other side housing the large vertical wheel adjacent Mr.

Neuman's gristmill. When she got there, a few men passed her by on their way home for the evening.

Although she felt sure she didn't really need to, Molly had been practicing her moves for weeks. Without much effort, she was already dancing rings around her brother Jake, her unwilling practice partner. Unable to keep her mind on anything else, Molly envisioned all the other young women's glowing acceptance of her, "the one they said didn't belong."

They will whisper, "'Did you see the way she carries herself, so graceful and sure? She's not just Enola's girl or Lil Mo anymore. And that dress, did you see it? That ocean-sea blue color seems to be flowing out with the tide. The fine lace and bodice are just exquisite. Where on earth could she have gotten such a gem of a costume?"Molly imagined.

Completely beside herself, Molly tightly wrapped her arms around her sides. She told herself this was part of the life she was born to experience. It was almost as if Molly recalled belonging to another time and place and somehow ended up here by mistake. Out of place, she'd always felt.

She knew sometimes ma thought her ways were strange. That's why she had almost broken down after the time ma told her to take it slow and not to expect so much from folks.

"But what else do I have, ma?" She'd said, pleading for answers.

"If I never go after my dreams, then it's like I never had any to begin with. So, what hope do I have?" She begged for understanding— getting no response.

"Before I was born, didn't our own President Lincoln say that everyone was equal? Mr. Temple told us in class that President Lincoln declared the proclamation to free all slaves in Mississippi and all the Southern states. But they didn't respond to the first order since the South was in rebellion. The Civil War was the beginning of the end of slavery and its one-drop rule. That's how much African blood made you a slave. Mr. Temple said that in September 1862, the president issued the first proclamation that announced that the emancipation was to take hold by that next year, on January 1, 1863," Molly had proudly shared with ma.

I can't help who I am and don't want to either.

She insisted, placing her finger in the water as it rippled through her mirror image.

Oh, I just get so mad when some ignorant coot has the nerve to treat me and mine like our president never uttered a word. Ma says, for my own sake, I had better just learn to control myself when people tell me what I can't be and can't say, or do.

All I have to do, Molly thought, *is to make sure that I don't allow anyone or anything to ignite that ire of mine. I don't believe my temper is really as bad as some say. And even if it is, well, I've got good reason,* she told herself.

No matter, I won't have to bother myself with those folks anymore, at least concerning this.

Molly assured herself as she stood up.

I don't expect they will ever try to box me in again, not like they tried before. Not after next week.

"I know where I belong," Molly affirmed loudly as she stared at her reflection on the lake. "And soon, so will everyone else."

Assured of things to come, Molly one step, two stepped, and dipped her way home, striding through the front door just as moonlit darkness set in.

****

Such is life. Molly had been crying for over two days. She had no idea why Jake was thinking about leaving them. Weren't they all staying? Jake didn't have to leave. He'd be no more a man up North than he was right here, she'd told him. Jake was the only one who shared with her what he could remember of their father. "It was not much, though, seeing that our pa had to leave in a hurry and never came back," Jake conceded.

"I think he was sad about it though," as Jake recalled. He was just a baby when his father left. The few times Molly tried to bring up the subject with ma, it always turned to other "more important things."

Yes, Jake was the only one who would share some of those secrets with her. Those things hidden, that she still didn't understand why—couldn't be spoken of.

Molly recalled the one that he told her when he thought she was old enough to understand, just last year. Ma still doesn't isn't aware that Molly knows, but why can't everyone know.

It made me beyond pleased. I think I always felt a connection. I was ecstatic when Jake told me. Mr. Neuman was good to everyone, but especially to us, now I knew why. The news had no real effect on my life, to the point where I had completely forgotten about the connection until many years later.

He began, "You know our pa? Well you couldn't remember him too well, but you know, I do. And well he was really, really white-looking.

He stopped for a moment to clear his throat, tugging at his collar.

"His mother was a slave, and he had a white man for a father, our pa did," he blurted out.

Molly remembered Jake saying that pa was almost white. He would say he was caramel colored like ma and that I got pa's coloring. She had always thought that was just something for Jake to say only to make talk.

"But that's not all, Molly", her brother had continued, "our pa's father was a relation of Mr. Neuman's."

At the time, she'd told Jake she didn't believe him, but he went on to explain exactly how Mr. Neuman's brother had come to America a long time before Mr. Neuman, and had different views about right and wrong than him. He added that several years after Mr. Neuman came to Grenada County, Mississippi he found out about his brother's child, who was about 25 years old at the time. He brought him here to work and live on the place, then signed papers to make him free. That's when ma came here, a freewoman looking for work, they met, got married and then they had us.

With everything Molly and Jake had shared, she just didn't understand why he wanted to leave now; but then again she did.

Maybe, she thought, Jake had been play-acting like her. There was so much more inside of that teasing, thoughtful, good-looking (she had to admit) frame than just working at the mill and around the farm.

Jake was top-notch with numbers and for two years running, Mr. Neuman asked for him to work on his books. Maybe Jake could use those skills now, to find a position up North, if people there were different, like she'd heard. If that's what he was thinking, then maybe him leaving is not so far-fetched.

Jake promised that he would write and that she was not to worry. He said that he was going to show Molly how it was done. Whatever that meant?!

Chapter Sixteen

The fall brought not only the rich lovely colors and the festival, but harvesting and memories of the previous year's Yellow Fever epidemic. The townspeople recalled that, "In the fall of 1878 Grenada was stricken by the greatest tragedy in the town's 40- year- history. On August 9, 1878 Dr. D.R. Brown, secretary of the Memphis Board of Health, [came] to Grenada to check on the rumored yellow fever. Dr. Brown confirmed the outbreak of this dreaded disease. By the time it was all over, yellow fever had claimed more than 350 lives in this town of two thousand people.

There had been some talk of canceling this year's Autumn Festival, but as the months passed, things began to slowly get back to as normal as possible. So many people in town had gotten sick and so many had died the year before. This year, 1879, everyone wanted to try to go on as normally as possible with their lives, especially those that worked for Mr. Neuman at the mill.

Walter Neuman's mill had been operating at full force now for 15 years. He was proud of it and had a right to be. Walter not only was responsible for its construction, but its total operation. He was an expert with controlling devices, the wheels, shafts, gear trains, and the knowledge of how to adjust his massive millstones to less than a wheat grains thickness apart. He had advanced technical knowledge necessary to milling more so than anyone in 50 counties. He was fortunate to have a good pond location immediately upstream of the mill dam. He operated what was called a "vertical mill" with a water wheel that consisted of a large metal wheel, with a number of blades or buckets arranged on the outside rim forming the driving surface. For all to see, the wheel was mounted vertically on the horizontal axle. Another wheel was positioned horizontally on a vertical shaft. The vertical wheel was the one that transmitted the power; through the axle and a ring gear and drive belts. Ultimately, the horizontal wheels directly drove the load of wheat or grain.

The mill employed more than one-tenth of the men in our town of 2,000 people. Many of those in neighboring Redding, Misterton, and Elliot counties also worked there. Mr. Neuman always gave first preference to his friends and closest neighbors, no matter what. He made a point of offering employment to several of the Freedmen over the last 10 years. He'd been a supporter of helping "the Negro" to become self-supporting American citizens after the war ended and the president proclaimed they were free.

Actually, the chief concern of Congress at this time — rather than the readmission to the Union of the Southern states — was the condition of the emancipated Negro. In March 1865, Congress established the Freedman's Bureau, to assume a position of guardianship over the Negro and direct his first efforts at self-support. In addition, Congress also formalized the fact of Negro freedom by proposing the 13th Constitutional Amendment which abolished slavery. It was ratified in December 1865.

During this time, Neuman also had the distinction of being the most accessible grain mill owner with the other being about 40 miles north of Hardy Station. And that one had been damaged during the "War Between the States". As in much of the South, the war caused a lot of damage in and near areas that came to be called Grenada County. Although hundreds of whites in the area were able to save most of their possessions, others lost their homes and many properties had been greatly damaged and had to be rebuilt where possible.

Walter recalled, "According to Mr. Jackson, that's what happened to his family home, but folks in town knew better."

Neuman's own farm managed to remain untouched by the sieges and skirmishes during those years.

Some believe it had to do with the respect the people on both sides of the issue had for the man.

Walter Neuman was unable to serve in the "War Between the States" due to an almost complete loss of hearing in his left ear as a child in Germany. He camouflaged it so well that no one knew about it until it kept him from serving in the war. What people didn't know, but suspected, was that this was fine with the man who didn't believe in the principles for which the South fought. He fully supported Lincoln from Illinois whom he voted for as president in 1860, despite his own state's succession.

However, Walter felt pity and sadness for many of his neighbors who'd lost their sons and husbands in the Vicksburg Campaign of 1863.

One week in particular Walter remembers crying like a baby when he received a short letter from one of his workers who began at the mill right after Walter opened it for business.

Camp near Yazoo River

July 20, 1863

Dear Mr. Neuman:

Thank you for sending me needed personal supplies when I know how you really feel about this "War Between the States." The campaign has now ended and the 73rd goes into camp with a small prospect of having one or two months rest. We have had about four months of very heavy campaigning during which time we have been in four or five skirmishes and have been about 6 weeks in the sieges of Vicksburg and Flowood. Since we left Statens's Bend, our regiment has lost several men killed in the siege of Vicksburg, 36 men died of disease, and 24 men wounded, 20 of them in the siege of Vicksburg and 4 of them in a skirmish near Canton.

Lieut. J.S. Moore

Even before receiving this disheartening letter, Walter had learned how, "Union General Grant won several victories around Vicksburg, Mississippi, the fortified city considered essential to the Union's plans to regain control of the Mississippi River.

On May 22, General Grant began a siege of the city. After six weeks, Confederate General John Pemberton surrendered, giving up the city and 30,000 men. The capture of Port Hudson, Louisiana, shortly thereafter placed the entire Mississippi River in Union hands. The Confederacy was split in two."

Walter remembered how Lena's father complained about his son-in-law's extremist ideas after he expressed his disappointment on arriving in America a year too late to travel to Lincoln's debates with Senator Douglas in Illinois.

Walter only wished that the differences in beliefs hadn't led to this destructive war and the South's secession.

What people respected and some hated about Walter Neuman was that the man was a friend and neighbor to every person who came across his path. There wasn't a neighbor during the hard years, or before and after the war, that he hadn't lent a hand of help and friendship.

The townspeople would reflect on all he'd do for anyone, and never playing favorites.

Many remembered just two years before, in August, there had been a terrible accident at the mill and a Choctaw worker lost his life.

Since then, Walter Neuman did everything needed to make sure he never lost another man due to equipment malfunction. He regularly called in experts, some from out- of- state, if needed, to inspect or repair any piece of machinery.

"Any one of my workers will be treated the same way that I would hope to be treated," he would say.

He also allowed his employees to have a familiarity with him. This did not always make him popular with many who believed that some were a few stations well below others. They felt Neuman was doing all those like him, especially themselves, an injustice— when he tried to put everyone on some kind of equal footing.

"Hey Neuman," Walter's foreman always addressed him as such, but this time he was almost shouting and looked fighting mad, "There's a problem over here with that new replacement piece we ordered a couple of years ago over in Duck Hill. The wooden and pinion gears keep grinding and getting stuck and won't power the millstone inside. It won't sieve the wheat at all once it gets to that point."

"What do you mean, Joe? I just had that machinery piece looked at only six months ago when we shut the mill down for over three weeks," Neuman replied, exasperated.

"I know," the foreman affirmed. "Why do you think I'm making such a big ruckus?"

"It will not be a problem for much longer— I will assure you of that," Neuman promised with a fierce look in his eyes.

The foreman took a step back, wondering what Neuman might do next. He was not a man to easily lose his temper, but when he did, look out and clear out.

****

Walter Neuman crossed the bridge and rode past Milcreek Pond in route to his home at the other end of his estate.

Entering in through the back door, he called for his companion, Ciaok, who had just recently returned from up North. Although Walter didn't want him to go, he'd left in 1872 to find better opportunities for himself.

"Ciaok, I want you to go into town and tele-graph this message to Leveret Equipment," he explained urgently.

While dictating the note, Walter took stock of the slightly older man's appearance.

He was concerned about how Ciaok had changed while away. As a young man, he'd shared with his employer and friend the details of how his people, the Choctaw, were the original owners of all the land in the territory now called Grenada County.

Since his return, Walter noticed how Ciaok's countenance had changed completely whenever he reflected on what had happened to so many of his ancestors. The atrocities of how so many were starved, slaughtered and run off their land.

Over the years Walter had learned as much as he could about his friends' people.

They were an Indian tribe that originally occupied Georgia, Alabama, Southern Mississippi, and Louisiana.

He learned the Choctaw were less warlike than their traditional enemies, the Chickasaw and the Creek. They lived in mud-and-bark cabins with thatched roofs.

They also were an agricultural people, probably the most able farmers of the Southeastern region, employing simple tools to raise corn, beans, sweet potatoes, pumpkins, and tobacco. They usually had a surplus to sell or trade.

Ciaok's people also raised cattle, fished, and hunted with blowguns and a bow and arrow. After the arrival of the Europeans, the Choctaw began riding horses and using them for pack animals.

Along with the Seminole and Chickasaw, the Choctaw developed their own horse breeds.

Over the last 150 years, the Choctaw had been forced to move farther and farther west to avoid conflict with the European settlers.

Walter learned that by 1842, they had ceded most of their land to the United States and were now mainly relocated in Indian Territory land set aside for them in Oklahoma.

At times now, the increasingly burdened Ciaok could be heard moaning over and over again, "We only tried to share and be friends, but they only wanted to lie to us. To cheat us. To kill us."

Once, Walter heard Ciaok rambling on about the possibility of his people being cursed because they were a slave-holding tribe. Walter listened to him pleading to his God for forgiveness for this, reminding his Maker that they had willingly offered to do penance for that human injustice. Cioak could be heard saying that it was not his will to be a slave holder and that he had rejoiced at the opportunity for his people to offer their "friends" long overdue land and money for all their help over the years.

Walter told himself he must remember to tread carefully these days with his trusted friend.

****

Despite his nurturing stance with his employees and friends, Walter could be relentless when necessary. And within one week, a systems man arrived on the new Union Pacific Railroad and all problems at the mill were resolved to Mr. Neuman's satisfaction.

This matter would have taken a month for anyone else to resolve, but not Walter Neuman.

Chapter Seventeen

Time was running short. In the midst of strong and blustery winds—which were preferable to stifling heat — Molly's shoes were to be gotten for the festival coming up in just over a week.

Except for two recent warmer days, the weeks earlier had been crisp and chillier than expected for this time of year. Molly noticed the leaves on some of the oak and pecan trees had begun to fall as she and ma climbed into the grey carriage and started on the road that early afternoon.

Everyone was grateful for these conditions, since the colder, early October weather quelled the chance for another terrible yellow fever outbreak. The final week in October, running over into November, had remained this way with a prediction of just a bit of warming up by the time of the festival

Keeping conversation with her mother, Molly remained proud that she was able to pay for the shoe order herself, despite Mr. Neuman's kind offer to pay and have her reimburse him long after the shoes arrived.

Yet, despite her denials — in response to her mother's earlier warnings about folk's displeasure— Molly was also feeling a bit panicky.

Nevertheless, with the sun high in the sky, she put her head out the carriage opening and inhaled its cool lemony rays. She then exhaled her mounting apprehension with every wheel turn of this not-too- rocky ride.

In no time, she and her mother embarked upon the outskirts of town; her mind fresh and emptied of all things negative. They arrived at the door of Mr. Richmond's shop at just after one in the afternoon.

As soon as they walked in, one look at old man Richmond's familiar weather-worn face, and Molly resigned herself to the fact that she knew exactly how he would react to their request to pick out and rush order dress shoes from the larger store copy of one Godley's Lady's Book.

Already irate over the tiny new mercantile that had opened up at the edge of town; Richmond blamed, "that danged Reconstruction and its Freedman's Bureau," for his current business losses. He and other proprietors had been fighting the competition by igniting old fears.

Old man Richmond decided to deal with the rivalry by fanning the flames of the past with sympathetic customers by proclaiming, "It just ain't seemly," hiding his real motives. "Those allowed to git so uppity."

Anticipating a problem herself, Enola took Molly aside and whispered something in her ear. Afterwards, Molly respectfully relented to her mother's wise discretion. Then Enola deliberately tiptoed over to old Mr. Richmond and began to recite something Molly could barely hear. What she did hear, near the end though, sounded like Mr. Neuman's name?

Richmond responded gruffly, his froglike face jutting forward with a sour thrust. He then backed over behind the counter, awkwardly reaching underneath, and snatched out a black box with the large book inside— slamming it on the counter.

"Ma," always the peacemaker, respectfully bought another small parcel to smooth things over. So all turned out well and the shoes were ordered. Still, the proprietor cut Molly and her mother a fierce glare, then slowly mouthed two words through gritted teeth that sounded and appeared to be "savage nig----" to the proud insightful girl.

Molly tried not to allow the tense scene to put a damper on her present euphoric state of mind.

However, she had her own choice words for old man Richmond as they were leaving.

But ma grabbed my arm before I could spit them out, she remembered.

Richmond reminded Molly of a caged rabid dog, chomping at the bit, who would pounce at any moment—if not for the cage.   How she longed to kick that "dog" right between the eyes, but Molly was not one for violence, not even towards such a "dangerous beast."

But, he deserves it, she glowered. He has no right to look at us like we were scum.

Still battling hurt protective feelings, for her mother even more than herself, Molly didn't realize her own strength. She had almost made a clean getaway, with temper intact, when she slammed the entry door to the store hard enough for the pane of glass to fall out and crash to the ground.

Enola turned to look at the damage and let out a slight gasp, as she dropped her parcel.

What she'd done, although unintentionally, didn't compare with this man's insulting ways with those who deserved better, the fair-minded girl believed.

At the moment, feeling vindicated she yelled, "The old ogre had it coming," without any regrets.

Before Enola could apologize for her daughter, Mr. Richmond ran outside, screaming through grinding teeth, "I'll see Neuman about this; yes I will, you- you cock-eyed, lap-legged..."

he spat out, as drool ran down the side of his mouth. Ending in mid-sentence, he picked up an old metal chair sitting outside the door, slamming it against the untouched pane—adding even more cracked, dangling glass to the pile below.

Enola firmly chastised Molly as she got back into the carriage and added, "Missy, that temper...did you ever think to wait until you had your shoes in hand, first, before you slammed that door and sounded off? You will never get them now!"

Molly cried out, "I never thought....Oh ma-mother do you think so? I didn't do it on purpose, not really. Should I go back and offer to pay for the window?"

"No," Enola stated. "It's too late for that, he'd kill you. I'll just have to explain to Mr. Neuman and he may have to get Ciaok to come back and pick up the shoes once, no, if they come in next week. You better pray long and hard that you can still get those shoes."

Molly sat unusually quiet on the trip back, glad the Neuman's driver was too new to already form an opinion of her from this latest mishap.

She had no idea what might happen with her shoes. This time she was sure she'd really done it!

Once back, Molly didn't wait around to see whether her mother headed over to the Neuman household to try and resolve what she felt sure was truly an accident.

After quickly darting like an arrow from the carriage towards the front door of the shanty, she pleaded towards the skies for some sign to rain down on her, "Oh God, please help me. What's wrong with me?"

Once inside, Molly ceremoniously pulled out the large black skillet and began washing and preparing the sliced fatback and bacon; plump, leafy collard greens and thick, buttery cornpone for dinner. She hoped to take her mother's mind off everything with the meal she, Jake, and ma enjoyed once, maybe once every other week.

There was no doubt in her mind that the meal tasted beyond delicious.   A few times, though, with all her reading up on everything, including food, she'd tried to "educate" her mother that the fatback and bacon weren't so good on the heart or their backsides. But she had to admit the rich pungent taste and crunchy texture of that pig after sizzling in ma's cast iron skillet was more than her beckoning appetite could resist.

Anyway, there was no way that Molly would take a chance on challenging the fates this day with any such talk.

Thoughts of what she'd done and ma's words remained on Molly's mind until Enola walked in a half an hour later to the smell of bacon frying and greens boiling in the big pot. The smell floated outside as her mother opened the door. Molly had expected that this would help smooth things over, but she knew it hadn't as soon as she turned and noticed the strange worried look on her mother's face.

"Mother, is everything okay?"

No response.

"Uh-uh, maybe just a bit better than before?" Molly questioned nervously, attempting, but failing at perfect diction.

With a blank stare, Enola looked down at the weathered wooden floor, yet didn't answer.

"Ma, what is it?" Molly asked a bit louder, forsaking caution for urgency.

Still silence.

This time, almost panicking now, Molly cried, "Ma...ma...please tell me what's the matter? I know I did wrong, I'm so sorry. Ma please forgive me!"

Enola finally directed a piercing stare at her daughter, and then answered, "Listen, you can't count on me to come running every time you get yourself in a spot."

"But, I didn't ask..."Molly began, and then stopped, thinking about how silly what she was going to say sounded.

After another long silence, Molly began calmly and deliberately, "I understand mother. I promised myself that I would get it right."

Enola added, "It's your only shortcoming, girl. Leastways it's the only one that I can see. But it's a big one."

Her mother continued, "What in the Sam Hill were you thinking, girl? Lord forgive me, but sometimes I think it would be better if you were homely, stuttered, or even crippled than you going off and losing your temper all the time."

Knowing how Molly's foot sometimes still stumbled, her mother's words really hurt. Enola's daughter couldn't remember when she'd seen her mother so disturbed. So much so that she was trembling.

"One day we won't be able to control what could happen to you at the hands of some people. Don't you understand girl!"

"Ma, what happened to you up at the Neuman house? Please tell me!" Molly demanded to know, now realizing something more had happened since the scene at Richmond's store that day.

With a pained expression, Enola slowly recounted how she first entered through the back door of the sprawling white house and found that Mr. Neuman was not at home. According to Ciaok, he had gone to Graysport Crossing, something about a problem at the mill. Enola was reluctant, but time was of the essence if Molly was to get those shoes in time for the festival, if at all. So she went to find Mrs. Neuman and explain the situation to her.

"She did what?" exclaimed Mrs. Neuman, who was not very sympathetic to Molly's perceived shortcomings as was her husband.

Enola swallowed her pride and suffered the humiliation of repeating what were the results of her daughter's outbursts this time.

Mrs. Neuman looked at Enola for what seemed like forever without uttering a word.

Then she grinned, almost as if she were enjoying "this little scene."

The lady of the house then began, "Enola, you know Molly is a danger to herself and the rest of your family as well. One day she will have to stand on her own, for her personal misdeeds. I just hope she makes it that long before someone finally gets their hands around her..."

"Excuse me madam," Enola stopped her employer's wife in mid-sentence. "I think it would be best if I take this up later with Mr. Neuman. When do you expect him, madam?"

"Why, don't you know?" She quipped.

Enola did not respond, seeing the mood the mistress of the house was in, she knew it was best.

Looking for someone to spar with, Lena Neuman condescendingly dismissed her longtime employee, "Yes, its best that you mosey along now, girl. Your cleaning is done for the day."

With that, the lady of the house strolled down the long hallway into the waiting parlor and gently shut the door behind her.

Chapter Eighteen

Walter Neuman walked through the mill to level his own inspection of his beloved workplace. Since he had built it with his own two hands—along with the help of hired townspeople and other paid workers— this had become the mirror of his determination to succeed. He wanted—no expected— and gave only the best. None of his workers went home complaining about this or that, because there was no reason. "Mr. Neuman" made sure they didn't; with his daily site visits every morning and afternoon. One never knew when he would show up; but when he did, everything had better be in top notch order and running smoothly. It's not that

Mr. Neuman was a cruel man, by any means. He was just no- nonsense. And if you wanted to be part of his "civilian infantry" you'd better fall in line or drop out.

****

The mill may have been the single most important place in Grenada County. It was in operation night and day. It provided flour from wheat for hundreds of people and was the only source of flour for everyone in the county and the surrounding area. The wheat was harvested and bundled as straw. It was then threshed, winnowed, and ground. The chaff and the wheat berry were separated. When the berry was cleaned of chaff it was ready to be ground into flour. Then the chaff was removed leaving the edible berry. Eventually the wheat was ground into flour on the millstone not once, but twice. The workers had to follow a multistep process within steps depending upon the machinery, cooperation of wind, water, and nature's elements to grow the wheat for harvesting. There were so many steps to the working of the mill that one had to be dedicated to learn them all. The process was expected to be studied and perfected for all who hoped to be a part of the team.

Some of the workers commented, "It's a shame the young men in that danged war didn't start out in this infantry as Neuman stock, heck we would have ended it in our favor, that's for sure."

Whenever talk of the war came up, there would always be a consensus. If you were from the South, you were expected to pull for the South, no matter what you really felt. You may not like all the ways of the South, but if you lived "here," you were a Southerner none-the-less, then you "darned well" better act like it. It didn't matter who you were, or what treatment you'd received now or in the past; it was "love" the South or "leave" the South. That was the consensus among all Southerners, "who mattered."

But when it came to the status quo, Walter Neuman was never a man to just fall in line. In the past, when talk came up at the mill about the war and how President Lincoln was handling the Union side, Mr. Neuman usually only listened without offering any comment. But the workers, along with everyone else around town, knew to leave well enough alone when it came to this "good man of status" and the thoughts that ran through his mind. As long as he remained a fine neighbor and a top-notch employer, no one was going to try to find fault and take on such a powerful man as an enemy. The few that had an idea of how Mr. Neuman's views ran, knew well enough not to share them with others.

Most believed, anyway, if you wanted to know what kind of a person a man was, all you had to do was watch him. And watch him they all did. He definitely was "something" to watch too, they believed. He was always doing some thing or another. If not buying up land or building a stellar house, then he was setting up the only wheat, corn, and grain mill in the state of Mississippi. It was the best run one in the entire South.

The sun came up with a vengeance that morning. Walter worried that it might get much too hot to expect the mill to operate extra hours that day. "I may have to let the men go at the regular time," he said to himself, as he entered the newly installed room in his home to wash and prepare for his long day ahead.

"I think I'll use this time to take another quick inspection of the workings of that repaired equipment," he murmured aloud as he took up his razor.

The owner worried that a few poorer farmers would still use the time to work their land, even if it was too hot— having so little time in the evening.

"Maybe it would be better to keep them at the mill where several ice blocks are stored and for their own good," he mused.

He walked back to his bedroom and paced back and forth. The air inside was kept cool by those same big ice blocks he kept at the mill. Without them, temperatures inside could reach almost 98 degrees during the summer months. He hadn't needed the ice blocks for a while except for a couple of recent warmer days, which were not nearly as bad. Mr. Neuman wondered how the people on his property made it in that summer heat. None were able to afford or store the ice blocks for cooling. In the past, he had attempted to get them sold smaller and cheaper to the men, but their pride was something fierce, and they wouldn't take what they called "charity" from anyone. So many found relief in the shade of the pine, pecan, or towering willow-oak trees surrounding Milcreek Pond and lining the countryside.

****

Walter came back home later that afternoon, after stopping at the mill to check on how the new equipment was holding up. He was pleased that the weather conditions did not turn hot as he'd expected that day. Once inside the door, Ciaok met him in the front hall.

Still his trusted friend, though his recent behavior was surely cause for concern, the dependable man told Walter of Enola's visit and what he had overheard.

After hearing the details according to Ciaok, Walter decided the best way to handle the situation would be to say nothing. He'd have Ciaok just pick up the shoes and bring them to the house next week. He'd have things smoothed over about the window with Richmond by then.

"That damned festival," Walter swore to himself, as he rarely did. He realized everyone was looking forward to his family sponsoring it this year. The other day he'd suffered through Jackson going on and on about how "nobody, just nobody, has turned the festival into a proper affair the way you have those last two years. Before the yellow fever canceled it last year."

"Before," he'd added, "it almost seemed just a step above the local barn dance. But well, words can't describe it now."

When Walter had gotten home that day, after listening to old Mr. Jackson, whom Walter was surprised still managed to attend such an affair; he asked his wife, "So what's the matter with a barn dance?"

"What barn dance" She cried. "Walter, I've explained that I'm getting final plans together for the Autumn Festival. I've also asked you if you have anything you would like to add to the event to make it even more spectacular and you mention a 'barn dance.'"

"Well, why not? Can't we tone things down a bit this year? Do we have to go all the way for the royal look?"

Lena's husband realized long ago that his wife, although from the North, had become a full-fledged Southerner. He even noticed that she could be mistaken for a supporter of the "Old South," a place he wanted no part of.

Not long ago, 'Men of means' were ruling over mass dependents. Here in the Old South, to be somebody wasn't hidden, it was shown by wealth displayed in great plantation homes and control over many heads.

To be a "gentleman" one had to sustain an appearance of distinction, this also called for an instantaneous response if insulted by anyone. Personal matters were taken care of by the people, never by the law or authorities. Duels were commonplace.

It was a place where "gentlemen" did not do a day's work, such as manual labor. However these "gents" had their daily chores: doing business, playing polo, giving instructions to overseers, to foremen, and listening to their wives' plans for festivities and parties.

But, to Walter, the worst aspect of being "gentlemen" was that they were the masters of other human beings. They prided themselves on knowing how to handle their slave property and make slaves submit to insults, or even disrespect themselves through acting like clowns. These "gentlemen" and masters had complete control and respect from all who depended on them.

Despite having arrived in America shortly before the war, Walter had learned a lot about life in the South's recent past. He could see that some of the old ways were kept intact, ways he believed should have ended with Lincoln's Emancipation Proclamation.

Lena knew his feelings about the subject and he was slowly becoming more aware of hers than even she knew or could hide from him.

"Walter, I just don't think you understand," his wife sighed.

"Maybe I don't," he sniffed. Walter Neuman had attended some of the annual fall festivals in the past and had to admit they were great fun. But people made too much out of looking just right; discussing what was to be worn and had been worn many months ahead and afterwards.

Even with his wealth, Walter always felt it didn't take a lot of money and buying everything in order to have a good time. But if that's what made them happy, well... he thought. Still, he had at least 30 fellows working for him who could well afford another job just to pay for the extra they had to spend for this event.

Walter guessed it didn't really hurt anyone, events like these, except possibly those who felt slighted for not being invited. At the last town meeting, he'd suggested that another family sponsor a less expensive and unpretentious dance for people who were uninvited or couldn't afford this one.

But, everyone at the meeting, surprisingly even those who couldn't afford the festival, agreed that the smaller folk dances in the spring and summer were more than enough to offset this one.

Lena broke in, "Dear, please understand at least one thing, we are sponsoring the festival again this year, period."

Walter added, "And I hope that this is the last time. This will be the third year now. Can't we allow some other family the responsibility of it next year?"

"How can you ask that," his wife questioned. "You know everyone looks forward to our sponsoring it now. Even Aunt Millicent is coming this year. Or I should say 'Aunt Minnie.' I don't know why she insists on being called by that ridiculous nickname. Millicent is so much more regal.

"Oh, by the way Walter, be sure to take the black coach to pick her up at the station.

"Anyway, she and everyone else expects us to host the festival. And what's the matter with that, I ask? You know we are not all so satisfied with everyday living. We want a taste of the good life once and a while."

"I take it you're referring to "the good life" you had in Maine before coming here, no less?"

"I didn't say one word about Maine," his wife retorted.

"Doesn't matter... I've heard enough to know when you're leading up to it." Walter replied, remembering how he used to admire her long-abandoned direct approach.

A knock on the door interrupted what was sure to progress into what the household staff called, the "Maine Melee."

"Yes?" Lena called out, curtly.

"Madam, there's a missus waiting for you downstairs in the parlor room," responded the servant meekly.

"Tell her I'll be right down." Mrs. Neuman responded, changing to her more cheerful tone.

"Walter dear, I'm going downstairs now to meet with someone to complete the final arrangements."

"Final arrangements, indeed!" he responded laughingly.

Finding no humor in him, she sighed, "Sometimes, Walter, I wonder if you will ever understand."

Disappointed, Lena walked out. Her husband stared at her solemnly; her silky alabaster neck glistening with sweet perfumed powder.

Although still lovely, he thought how much that stunning, direct young lady had changed, in so many ways, over the years.

Walter's words trailed after Lena as he murmured in a low voice, "I understand a lot more than you think my lovely wife."

Chapter Nineteen

Molly felt she hadn't found out everything that had happened that afternoon with her mother up at the Neuman house. But everything seemed to be resolved. One evening, a week later, Ciaok delivered her shoes to the door of their shanty. When the shoes arrived Molly recaptured her latent fervor over what was to come. After polishing them for the third time and holding the shoes up against her gown for the tenth, her mother finally demanded that she make herself scarce for a while.

Shaking off the last remnants of guilt about everything, Molly did just that. She gyrated her trim shapely figure to the slightly staccato rhythm of her heart as she made her way down the path towards her "safe haven" before the sun went down that evening. As Molly swayed on, her one and only male admirer came toward her, appearing like a shadow from behind one of the rustling willow-oak trees.

"Haven't seen you in a while," Molly declared lightly.

The two sat down on an oversized log near the lake's edge. Alex listened while Molly began to bubble over discussing the upcoming event. She paused to take a breath, leaving an uneasy silence, as the young couple peered at the setting sun sliding across Milcreek pond where it adjoined the gristmill on the Neuman farm.

"I'm not going, to the festival, I mean," Alex broke in, matter-of-factly.

"How come?" Molly tried not to sound utterly heartbroken, since she had hardly seen him in the past two months.

"It's only for folks looking for a show or looking to show-off," he accused.

"That's not so," Molly shouted defensively.

Alex didn't respond right away.

They both turned away from each other and Molly purposely fixed her gaze on two barn swallows flying overhead towards their resting place for the night.

"You don't need to get all fired-up, Molly, it just ain't important to me, that's all," he almost apologized.

"Oh well, that's okay," Molly said, now looking at him. She lied.

"But I wish you were going," she then added truthfully.

"At least you can come by and see me before I leave. I will be a true vision, you know that," she smiled confidently.

"You're already somethin' to me, right now," Alex added shyly, giving her his full attention.

Molly blushed at what she believed to be a direct compliment from her one and only suitor. She wasn't used to Alex being so forward with her. But he wasn't so direct as to be insulting, so she didn't feel the urge to slap him or anything. But, still, she didn't think ma would approve of such talk.

Purposely looking away and noting the sky suddenly darkening, Molly welcomed an excuse to change the subject.

"Alex, looking at that sky reminds me of a story, did you ever hear how this spot got to be called Milcreek Pond?" She asked abruptly.

Taken off guard, but not discouraged, Alex tensed his thick neck muscles, and coolly moved his head slowly from left to right in response.

Playing along, he pointed out that the opaque shimmering waters, which had mirrored the clear evening sky, had changed as swarthy clouds rolled in.

The two sat quietly among tall prairie cord grass mingled with cattails swaying fiercely along the edge competing for space with white sun-flowers whose pale petals reflected the emerging mood overhead.

The whole atmosphere inhaled and exhaled fiercely as the breeze whipped back and forth.

Identifying with nature's sudden force, Alex had the urge to take just a bit more liberty.

Turning and gazing into Molly's hazel brown eyes, he took her hand and beckoned pleadingly, "Molly, truth be told. Is this really what you wont to talk about right now, I mean?"

"I think it is," she replied, pulling away her moist palm, and the tempting conversation that her own awakening longed for.

"It went unnamed, Milcreek Pond did," she pressed on, "until Mr. Neuman got this land and built it up, along with the new mill years ago. I believe it was a little less than twenty years or so.

"People used to believe the woods were spooked with 'lost souls' crying out in the night floating in the thick forest brush. Everyone would steer clear of this land then. It's hard to believe this place could ever be a cause of fear for anyone, don't you think?"

While talking to Alex she left out the time Jake told her that ma had mentioned some terri-ble things happened to people in those woods years ago. Things too terrible to talk about... She knew some of the stories of the past.

I'm not as naive about such matters as every-one believes.

But, even though, I knew, I didn't want to hear it anymore! The past is past. That's how I have to look at it.

Along with scary talk of the past, the threatening clouds passed, the winds died down, and dusk fell uneventfully. Molly stared at the last sign of light as it ceased to shimmer across the lake.

A huge sinister looking raccoon, growling and snarling like a masked bandit, scurried across in front of them when the creature believed it to be dark enough to venture out from the woods.

Molly watched closely as he tethered along the edge trying to avoid falling into the water, using the whole sole of his foot "heel to toe" as he walked, now steadying himself on a narrow log situated between two old canoes.

She and Alex both let loose an ebullient howl, letting go of the evening's tension, giving more emotion than the unsuspecting animal's uneasy balancing act called for.

"Don't you worry", Alex sputtered, "Swimming comes easy to them raccoons, they uses water for hunting and they have been known to drown a dog or two."

Molly could not stop laughing. Yet the creature's deliberate, careful movements did somehow manage to remind her of herself and that two-step waltz she'd been practicing painstakingly for last few days.

"Hopefully," she cried aloud, "I'll do a whole lot better than he just did."

Chapter Twenty

"Aunt Minnie! Welcome, it's so marvelous to have you here. It's been almost three years since we last saw one another. And don't you look wonderful," Lena Neuman announced, as she took in her aunt's smart-cut traveling outfit.

"I don't look wonderful at all, I'm hot, dusty and I need a cool bath. So dispense with the formalities my dear and give your ole,' well not-so old, aunt a hug and kiss on the cheek."

The stout unpretentious older woman reached out and embraced her niece tightly around her slim shoulders.

Molly had a clear view of the pair and could also hear them from the upstairs bedroom window. This "aunt" was all that everyone said she was. She could tell from here that there was no fakery in this take-charge lady. She must have been a force to reckon with in her day, Molly thought.

As the long awaited guest turned to go in, alert eyes caught curious ones staring down at her stylish traveling bags being carried in by Ciaok.

"Who is that pretty little thing peering from the bedroom window," she asked her niece.

Already knowing, Lena Neuman looked up into the intent gaze of the troublesome girl with whom she had no patience. "Oh, that's Molly. She helps out with her mother during the week. She is always watching someone or doing something when she should be working."

As Mrs. Neuman and her aunt walked in to the house behind Ciaok, the mistress of the house told him to have Molly come downstairs.

Watching the young girl carefully step down into the front hall, Lena began, "Molly, go and see if your mother has more chores for you to complete."

"Yes, Mrs. Neuman madam," Molly replied dutifully, giving an exaggerated curtsy to the floor as she backed away towards the kitchen.

The lady of the house though, didn't find it at all humorous, but somehow disrespectful. Not much to her surprise, though, her aunt found the girl to be quite comical and spirited.

"So the pretty little one is quite a handful, I take it?"

"You are quite correct," Mrs. Neuman rolled her eyes and sighed, "I ignore her at every turn."

Molly walked into the kitchen to find her mother putting away the breakfast plates.

"Molly, I heard Mrs. Neuman send you in here. I hope everything is okay. Nothing wrong?" Her mother asked.

"No, ma. She just wants some time with Aunt Minnie in the parlor without me in the way, that's all," Molly said, attempting to ease her mother's fears.

"Why would that be," Enola questioned," I would think her aunt would like to go straight to her room to freshen up a bit after such a long trip. Molly are you sure?"

The girl exclaimed, "Yes ma, I'm very sure. What other reason is there except she wants you to find more work for me to do. I know she doesn't like me, ma. She's always at me."

Not intending on going down that road again, Enola stated firmly, "It is of no never mind if she likes you or not, she may be tiring of you talking, instead of when you should be working."

"That's not fair, ma, you know I never slump off. You know I finish all my work here. I'm very grateful to Mr. Neuman for this job and the wages," Molly responded, feeling hurt.

"Well you had better show just how grateful you are, and that means to the lady of the house, too," her mother warned.

"But I try, ma. I try to be nice and respectful, but she won't let me. She won't even look at me, just orders me around." Molly pleaded for some understanding.

"I tell you again, it's no matter." Enola ended the discussion on that note and Molly knew it was over.

"Take those extra towels up to Ms. Millicent's room. And let me tell you now, don't you ever let me hear you call her Aunt Minnie again," Enola warned her daughter.

****

Millicent Grandville enjoyed the long trip more than anyone would have suspected. She hadn't been out and away from Boston since her husband Albert died two years ago. Life got boring and she felt in a continuous rut. She felt her grieving period was over, and it was time to tackle life again. This ball coming up would be just the thing to get her back to her old self.

A knock on the door brought the older woman back to her present surroundings. The pale, yellow satin wallpaper and a delicately embroidered bedspread with matching white chintz curtains she liked so much. She and Albert had stayed here, right in this room, each time they visited with Lena and Walter.

Having knocked twice, Molly felt she waited for what seemed like hours for Ms. Neuman's aunt to answer. Molly was sure that she was to stay in this particular room. Maybe someone moved her and forgot to tell ma, she wondered anxiously.

As Molly turned to walk away she heard a robust, "Come in. Come in."

Slowly entering, Molly had it uppermost in her mind to take painstakingly great care to act as respectful as she knew how.

"Welcome. Good day, madam," she spoke in whispers, holding her head down. "I brought your towels."

Millicent chuckled, "Well if it isn't the pretty little thing from the parlor."

"Yes madam," Molly nodded, unsure of how to respond correctly to such a statement.

"Yes madam, that's it?" She pretended to be disappointed. "So reserved, that's a change from what I saw downstairs."

"Yes madam, I know," Molly continued, determined to harness her genuine self, as she was told.

"Well, if that's how you're going to be," the woman feigned hurt feelings, "then come and help me pick out some things for dinner."

Millicent Grandville decided that the spirited girl must have been reprimanded for her earlier display outside the parlor. The child had to adhere to the South's right and wrong code of behavior to survive, she suspected.

Well Aunt Minnie was here, and she had her own rules. She liked the girl who wasn't purposely disrespectful, just a lively young thing, no more, no less.

Molly followed this peculiar acting woman to her closet where a girl had already hung her dresses. The woman slid back both of the double doors and there before Molly's eyes, in some of the most exquisite colors, were the most alluring silk, satin, and lace dresses she'd ever seen. Among them: a soft silky carrot-colored orange; another bold pear-green, edged with lace; and most lovely, a satin royal blue with a white bodice in a shade of white that Molly didn't recognize at all. The young girl couldn't stop staring.

Although she was in complete awe and wanted to say so much, she had been warned.

"How exqui... I mean nice," she managed to sputter.

Aunt Minnie finally laughed out loud at the girl's deliberate show to contain her enthusiasm.

"Okay, little one, why are you trying so hard not to show how you really feel?" She asked knowingly.

Molly wasn't sure how to answer. But slowly, she began to believe that she could trust this strange woman with her secret.

"You never have lived around here, Mrs. Grandville, madam," Molly began, "I'm not sure you'd understand."

Millicent paused. No, she hadn't forgotten where she was. Over the years, she had become accustomed to the prim acting, proper speaking, finishing-school girls in Boston. It was refreshing to find a bright-eyed spitfire who seemed to be bursting with excitement and mischief. She was sure she'd discovered that in this pretty little thing.

Molly looked away from the woman's furrowed brow towards the closet. The alluring gowns seemed to call out for her undivided attention.

"Go ahead, my dear, you may take a closer look at them." Aunt Minnie offered as she took a gown off its satin hanger, "Feel the fabric, hold it in your arms."

Molly was sure she was dreaming and would wake up right then. But she didn't. In her open arms lay the most breathtakingly magnificent gown she'd ever seen.

"What color is this bodice?" Molly dared to ask.

"It's called lemon alabaster; this is the one I'm wearing to the Autumn Festival." Aunt Minnie added, "Are you coming to the festival, little one."

Molly was still stroking the beautiful satin gown as she replied, "Yes, madam."

"You don't have to keep calling me madam. Call me Aunt Minnie," the woman insisted.

Remembering what ma said, the girl's eyebrows shot up almost to her soft chestnut brown hairline at the thought of calling a relative of Mrs. Neuman's, aunt anything.

"I'm not sure everyone would be happy if I did that madam." Molly said knowingly.

Millicent could see her point. "Yes, I think you're right about that," she agreed.

How can one get used to this place? She thought.

"Well you can still call me Aunt Minnie when we're alone," she winked.

Molly smiled conspiratorially, "I'll try. I just hope I don't make a mistake and let anyone else hear me, madam. I mean Aunt Minnie."

"That's it, good girl!" Then the woman added, "So you say you are going to the festival, miss pretty."

Molly didn't mind the nickname. With some people she would have thought they were trying to make fun. It's not that Molly thought she was homely, quite the opposite, it was just that people never say much about how she looks. They just stare at her a lot.

"Yes, M... Aunt Minnie, I have a new dress just for the festival this year. I'm so excited I can't think of anything else."

Slowly, Molly began to open up like a sun-kissed flower in the spring with her new-found "friend."

"A new dress?" Aunt Minnie repeated, clasping her hands together in anticipation, "I would love to see it."

Although she was aware it paled in comparison to the gowns in "Aunt Minnie's" closet, Molly described the dress that she was, and still is, so very proud of.

167

"Oh, how enchanting it sounds, my dear. Your youth and loveliness will drown out everyone else in this gown of yours. You don't need a wagonload of embellishments like some of us do," she assured this shining beauty of a girl.

Molly was grateful for Aunt Minnie's attempt to make her feel good about her own less glamorous dress. She couldn't have known that the woman's comments were the honest truth.

Millicent Grandville lifted her gown from the bed and hung it back up.

Turning towards Molly who was admiring the chic cut of Millicent's salt and pepper gray hair, she asked, "Help me pick out something less attention grabbing for dinner tonight.

"How about this canary, yellow, little two-piece frock," she asked the girl, pulling out the attractive suit.

"It's perfect" Molly agreed, reaching to stroke the lace collar. She had lost all of her guarded reserve with this wonderful woman.

"I need to hurry back to help ma, now, before she comes looking for me," the young girl suddenly remembered as she moved toward the bedroom door.

Before she could reach it, however, a soft but insistent knock halted her retreat. She opened the door and there stood her mother, with a stern look on her face, waiting to escort Molly back downstairs.

Understanding the situation, Millicent offered support. "Thanks for all your help Molly," she called out, remembering to dispense with the girl's new nickname.

"Yes, thank you, Au... madam," Molly toned down her beaming smile, relishing their shared secret.

Molly's mother shook her head as they both made their way back downstairs. Enola wondered if she didn't almost hear what she thought she heard. Why hadn't she just warned the child only thirty minutes ago?

She sighed.

Not oblivious to her mother's peril, Molly restrained herself from sliding down the polished railing of the winding staircase with unbridled anticipation of secrets to be shared with this unusual confidant.

Twenty-One

That very next day, Molly saw Aunt Minnie stroll in from beyond the garden, then head out in the direction of Milcreek Pond. Molly followed not far behind, embracing the scent of fresh jasmine the woman left behind, as she now hurried along the path which led to the other "estate" that Molly would like to forget.

Molly hadn't been back there since she had that "run-in" a while back with the "old maid" as she liked to call her.

What would a grand lady like that want with that bunch over there? Molly wondered.

She was also curious about why ma seemed so nervous about Mrs. Neuman's aunt coming to visit in the first place. They'd had guests before, just a couple of months ago, as a matter of fact.

Molly tried to forget that too.

No reason to worry, she reassured herself.

Aunt Minnie was by far the nicest female she'd ever met, next to ma, of course, she told herself, without question.

****

On the third day of her aunt's visit, Lena Neuman decided to approach her about taking up permanent residence with them. Although she'd notified Enola months ago to make room for her aunt's permanent stay, she had never brought up the issue with her own aunt or even her husband, until now.

"Aunt Minnie, you know how much Walter and I would love to have you live here with us," she began.

"Lena, I realize that and don't think I don't appreciate it, but you and Walter don't need an old widow like me in the way," her aunt chided, hoping for agreement.

"Why that's absolute nonsense, auntie," Lena responded, sounding taken aback, "You'd never be in the way. I realize, though, that you would want your own place, a space of your own, right?"

"I'm not understanding what you're getting at, dear," Millicent smiled at her now slightly anxious niece.

Lena continued, putting her needlepoint to the side, "I mean you would stay here if you could have a place to call your own. A place designed just for you, cottage-like... Oh darling, I know how much you loved that quaint home you and Uncle Albert had when you were younger and..."

Millicent interrupted, "You don't mean that place, the ivy covered brick one with the white shutters, do you? I could never forget how much in love we were there."

"Yes, auntie, I remember the stories you used to tell, and just think, you can re-live those times again. Walter and I can make the sweet memories come alive again. We can duplicate that cottage for you," Lena grew more animated seeing her aunt's pleasure.

"I remember," she pressed on, "that snowy winter when I stayed with you for a few weeks. I was an idealistic, headstrong young girl back then. Some evenings we'd lay across that tickly bear rug by the toasty stone-etched fireplace. I would be gazing out of those two side wooden-paneled rectangle shaped windows with the checkerboard panes and the big centered picture window, and we'd both be humming along to Bach. The white crystals would still ice up on the outside corners of the panes, despite the warmth of the fireplace and the floating aroma of your

apple turnovers. The sound of the crackling but-
ter from pan to the oven produced those glistening, brown flaky crusts that I managed to sneak
out of the kitchen. Sliding sweet, chunky morsels
over my scorched tongue before they could cool,
I was in heaven."

"I recall you thought I didn't see you, but I
could hear you. That's what you got for not waiting until they cooled." Her aunt winked.

"I always wondered. I did manage to steal a
few." Lena laughed.

"That was so long ago, and me moving here,
dear, isn't that asking a lot?" her aunt questioned.

"And where would the house be located.
You'd have to have one built. There are no available cottages like that, at least not around here.

"Oh," she calmly added, "We can handle
that."

"But it would take a while to have one built,
wouldn't it?" Millicent wondered aloud.

"Oh, there will be one available very soon, the
best one on the estate. It will only need an addition or two and some sprucing up," Lena assured
her.

"Lena...you're not going to put some poor
family out to make room for me, are you? Millicent demanded to know.

"It doesn't matter," Lena answered without
emotion.

"Yes it does! Who would you just put out
that way? I wouldn't do someone's dog in such a

manner." Millicent hoped to evoke some feeling from her niece.

"Their dog, no," Lena responded with even less care, "Neither would I. Pets are special."

Millicent Grandville and Lena Neuman sat presently staring at one another for what seemed like a lifetime. One was wondering if she ever really knew the other, while the other was intent on accomplishing her mission, no matter what it took.

Finally Lena broke the silence. "Well, Auntie, if you must know, it's that Enola and her unruly daughter. Her son, who was not a problem, is gone now, and they are having a hard time keeping the place up," she concluded.

"Why, I never heard of such?" How long have they been in there?" Her aunt questioned.

"I don't remember and it doesn't matter, anyway. My only concern is getting you here and keeping you happy," Lena smiled broadly.

"But I won't be happy if you put that family out on the road," Millicent assured her.

"Oh they won't be put out on any road. I'm sure they will be fine. And it's as I said, with her son gone, the woman can't keep up the place. She would be happy for a way out," Lena replied, trying to sound convincing.

"Never mind, Lena. It's out of the question. I will stay in Boston, I'm really quite happy there." Millicent continued, "Also, I now recall that Enola and her family have lived in that house for over 16 years.

Do you actually believe she and her family would be fine? Don't tell me you believe that they can go anywhere and get the life they have here now. She and her daughter both work for you in the house here, don't they?"

"Aunt Minnie, you worry too much. You're such a kind, loving soul that people take advantage of your good nature." Lena cajoled, reaching for her aunt's hand.

"Just let me take care of the details and relieve your fears. I promise you that Enola and the girl can take care of themselves. They'll be just fine."

"I don't know how you came to be such a cold, cruel women Lena, you were never this way as a girl, but I won't discuss this with you any longer."

Seeking an end to the heated conversation, Millicent bolted upright— causing her niece's hand to slip onto the chair.

Offended at her aunt's chastisement and her response to what Lena felt was a very gracious offer, she took to attacking what she believed to be her "precious" aunt's, "abolitionist-like" attitude.

Slavery was over in the south. No one needed her aunt's protection.

" Hold on, auntie", she stopped her aunt, before she could step away, " you may not seem like me, but I'm positive you rode on one of those plush, black walnut Pullman coaches with the padded velvet seats and lighted chandeliers. You snuggled in a cozy bed as well. Don't tell me you didn't have those Pullman porters at your beck and call, satisfying your every whim. How was it relaxing in those mahogany and oak cars with etchings on the glass doors and gas lit chandeliers. Those cars even have hot running water, better than most of the houses out this way. It seems to me that you, dear auntie, sympathize way too much with people you'd never want to live like or with."

That may be so Lena, but it isn't the whole truth, and it has nothing to do with putting someone out of their home.

Lena went on, "Did you eat in the dining car or the buffet car, auntie?"

Ignoring her aunt's grim expression, the younger woman leaned back to a reclining position, folded her arms, crossed her legs, then sweetly added;

"Did you invite some of your fellow passengers from second class or even third class to plop down their day's wages for just one meal? Just one meal, auntie?"

There was a long silence in which neither woman spoke.

But Lena, determined to hold on to the last word and ultimately have her way, reached out again, this playing peacemaker, "Okay, dear, maybe I was wrong, we'll talk again later."

Standing motionless, unable to look at her niece sitting right in front of her, Aunt Minnie swiftly brushed past, rushed toward the door, leaving her niece still seated, and turning to stare at her aunt's retreating figure.

Lena had planned on using her aunt's agreement with the idea to plead her case with Walter. Although she'd told Enola months ago that both she and Walter had agreed that their family must move so her aunt could have the house, Lena knew that he would be completely against it. But she counted on his affection for her aunt— so recently widowed— and believed everything would finally come to pass.

Now with this delay, she decided—picking up her needlepoint pattern— to put the mission off until after the festival.

All of her attentions must be focused on making this year's festival the year to be remembered. Taking this as her cue, she put away her sewing and moved to her dressing table, touching the corners of her perfectly coiffured hair. She then headed downstairs to find her aunt and to smooth things over with her.

****

During the week, Molly noticed that Aunt Minnie had gone over to the Jackson "estate' a total of four times since she'd first arrived in town. Although the girl had vowed to be "totally respectful" and "good," always minding her own business—this was different, she believed.

That evening she approached her mother while she prepared pinto beans and ham for the week's special meal.

"Mother," Molly started primly, "Did you know that Miss Millicent visits the Jackson place a lot?"

Enola knew trouble was coming when her willful daughter began with "mother" instead of "ma."

Molly waited for her mother to answer. After a long silence, she could tell no response was forthcoming, so she continued.

"I saw her walking down the road earlier this week and at least three more times since. She always goes past Milcreek Pond and through the trees to the Jackson place.

Molly paused again, waiting for a response.

"Well I just wondered," she went on, "not that I'm being noisy, because I'm not. You know I've been minding my own business lately, at least these last couple of weeks, anyway."

Enola finally decided to put a stop to her daughter's prying with one well-placed word.

"Enough!" she bellowed.

Molly instantly silenced herself; duly fearful of what was to come next.

After a long pause, Enola almost whispered, "Molly, I'm not sure if you are deliberately trying to ruin your life or not. Because I love you more than my own life, I will remind you one last time.

"MIND YOUR OWN BUSINESS!" She abruptly shouted, taking the startled girl aback so much so that she grabbed a nearby chair to balance herself.

Molly was crushed. Her mother had never raised her voice to her in this way. Tears streamed down, as she put her slim hands over her face.

Enola would not be swayed. For her daughter's own good, she believed, she stayed strong.

"I don't think you are minding your own business at all, Molly. There could be a lot of reasons why Ms. Millicent choose to visit the Jackson place, but that's her business not ours," she pressed on; "Do you understand?"

"Yes, madam," Molly started up again, despite her tears, "B...But, you s-see, I tried to think of some reasons and I couldn't—n-not one. The Jacksons act n-nothing like her. I can't understand it and it bothers me. W-What would they have to say to each other?"

Enola tried not to get even more upset. She now believed that this daughter of hers actually could not stop herself. It was like Molly once said, like she was placed here out of some other time, or another place, and with no understanding of life as it exists in this one.

There was nothing Enola could do but love her, pray for her, and watch in silence as she suffered the consequences of her natural curiosity and impatience with this life.

Vowing to resolve herself as best as she could, Enola responded calmly this time to Molly's questions. "First of all, Molly, you don't know everything about people. Don't believe you do. You've only helped Ms. Millicent with her hair and clothes every day. That doesn't mean you know everything about her."

Molly thoroughly wiped her tears away, perking up at her mother's instant change in attitude.

"But I do much more than that, ma. We talk. She's told me all about her life, her dreams... everything," Molly insisted naively. For a moment, she had forgotten their secret pact.

"That's okay Molly, but I'm positive she has not told you everything about herself, okay?" Enola assured her innocent daughter. "Now what about that festival of yours, my girl?" she reminded her.

Twenty-Two

The morning of the autumn festival had arrived. Without having to get ma's permission to ask for it, Mr. Neuman offered to give Molly the Saturday morning off. Molly had gotten a peek at the ballroom and terrace the day before. She felt her limited words could not do justice to what she had seen.

This year the ballroom was decorated in a French provincial theme. The Neuman's had researched the rich French cultural heritage in preparation. It was modeled out of the Château de Bourdeilles— an ideal historic setting for so many with French ancestry and relatives in the South.

To complement the theme, the ladies dresses, this year, would be like "none we've ever seen," Molly overheard Mrs. Neuman say. Molly then learned that one of Mrs. Neuman's garden party club ladies, the Lady De Matthew, was to wear a gown by the famous designer for English nobility. Later into the evening there would be a concerto solo by a famed pianist.

Glancing up at the clear evening sky, Molly approached the front of the grand house. This time as a guest. She glided through the large entry doors into the glorious front hall. The sparkling chandelier drew her attention. She looked up toward the ceiling trying to erase the image of her mother on the high ladder, dusting it, from her mind. This would be her night, the commencement of her future had now begun.

While surveying the room, Molly was happy to see a familiar face in Mr. Neuman's trusted employee and friend. "Good evening, Ciaok," Molly called.

For several years, he'd chosen not to attend the festival as a guest, though he had every opportunity to do so.

"Molly, you are looking so grand. I'm speechless," he smiled.

"Thank you, Ciaok." I am feeling rather self-assured this evening. You don't think it's too understated?"

"With your beauty," he winked lovingly, knowing Molly since a babe, "too much jewelry and lace would have surely taken away from it."

With that encouragement, Molly continued to sway   confidently towards the resplendently elegant ballroom, which led out to the terrace and upper balcony. As Molly entered the room she had to catch her breath. The French decor was even more exciting to her, now that she could see all the people enjoying the setting.

Several appreciative glances turned in her direction as the soft blue satin hem of her gown swept the polished marble floor. Her hair, done up in a chignon, with tendrils cascading down the side of her oval shaped face, was ornamented with shades of blue and white satin ribbon to complement the shimmering satin and lace of her gown. Molly had been so thrilled when ma surprised her with a tiny box-shaped looking glass for the wall in their room—just to view herself on this special occasion.

Still conscious of the stares, Molly's mind reverted back to the other evening. How she wished Alex had decided to come or at least stop by, as he'd promised.

Although he was becoming part of her life these days, she had hoped that he would also be a part of the new life she'd set out for herself. He had shared his hopes and plans for the future and she had been sure they were attempting to travel in the same direction.

But on the way home the other evening, Alex finally confessed to her, "Molly... are you sho' you really want me to court ya...with this here ball shindig and yo' proper training and all?   I just don't reckon I'm gonna be good enough for ya."

"No matter…"You say fetch, I say carry. We'll work on it," Molly told Alex.

Seeing he was still unconvinced, Molly assured him as only she could: "Alex…have you seen yourself in the looking-glass lately?" She asked.

It seemed Alex didn't think that he needed to travel the route that Molly wanted to take in order to get to where he wanted to go in life. But this mission was not a deliberate task or a chore for her, she told him. This was a glorious wonderful experience. It was her real life, the life Molly felt she was always a part of, but was kept away from. She felt welcomed and at home. She tried to make him understand.

Molly's thoughts were interrupted by a vaguely familiar face— one whose name she couldn't seem to recall.

"Hello Molly." I must say you look as if you were born to wear that gown. You actually took my breath away when I first saw you come through the doorway. Do you realize that you are the most appealing young lady in this room?" The attractive gentleman flirted.

Molly was not used to such attention, especially from someone whose name she could not even remember. She stood speechless, staring blankly.

"I'm sorry, I've left you dumbfounded," the handsome stranger apologized. You don't remember me do you? I'm John Wagner, Walt Neuman's nephew. I was here just last year to help during the yellow fever epidemic. You were just turning 14 then, and I, an old man of 28, why should you have remembered?"

Now, Molly *did* remember him and remembered him well. He was tall, at least six foot one. Unlike Mr. Neuman, his hair was black and thick, combed across a high, broad forehead and just above deep dark brown eyes. His complexion was more of an olive coloring than anything else. She thought he had a kind of gypsy look about him. She remembered wishing she could have been a lot older, so he might have paid some special attention to her. Ma had mentioned hearing Mr. Neuman talk about the family being so proud of him for finishing medical school so young.

Before she could respond, an older heavily jeweled woman in dark gray taffeta—loudly clearing her throat first— called from across the room.

"Dr. Wagner, would you please come over? I have a few 'special' people I'd like for you to meet."

Sighing heavily, Dr. Wagner was visibly dismayed at the untimely interruption. But before stepping away, he said, "I'd like to claim a waltz, later, if that is acceptable."

Molly who had yet to find her voice, sputtered,

"Yes, by all means. I would be very happy to save you a waltz."

"I'm honored, beautiful lady." With that, he turned and strolled toward the waiting group of onlookers.

Molly trembled at now receiving the special attention, again remembering how Dr. Wagner, Mr. Neuman's sister's son, came down to help out last year. He told ma that his mother had come to America several years after her younger brother, but settled up North and married Dr. Henry Wagner, the young doctor's father, shortly after arriving.

****

Now left standing alone, Molly was wondering how she was going to "fire up" the evening. Here was her first encounter. And she had been nervous and almost totally speechless. Where was all her fine talk she had been learning for over a year now? It was all there and a part of her, she knew it.

Just relax.

She told herself.

Let it out.

This was an evening she had been waiting for all her life. To enjoy and be enjoyed— to release the girl in the reflection.

"Otherwise, they will never get to know the real you," she whispered to her mirror image.

Confidence now in tow, she turned to see a few sharecroppers' daughters, some mothers of the children she taught, and women she'd passed on the road to town from time to time; all talking to one another off to the side and staring in her direction. The large group also included share-cropper's wives from several of the neighboring estates who had saved enough to afford this eventful evening. Molly even recognized quite a few of the older girls from school, and thought it best to go over and just mingle a bit. However, she had no intention of staying in that corner with all of them for more than a moment or two.

As Molly walked over, a few began to smile and compliment her dress, while others stared blankly, pursed their lips, or even twisted their mouths into an off-putting scowl.

"Hey, Miss Molly," called out one lady.

Molly could not recall her name.

Without warning, she spewed out sarcastically, "My, My...don't you look just grand. A right lady of the house, that's what YOU are. Prancing around..."

Then an older girl, in a dark yellow taffeta castoff, whom Molly had tangled with while in school and who couldn't seem to master anything at all in class, croaked, " Hey Mo, wudn't that Doc Wagner, Mistah Neuman's nepfew you was over there wit. What in the tar nation would he be wuntin' wit chew wit that game leg of yours?"

Struggling to keep a straight face, showing no reaction to their taunts, Molly could see that they had no intention of being friendly at all—and she was in no mood for a battle with them tonight.

If they felt like they didn't belong, and wanted to stay in that corner, criticize and gossip; then why did they come anyway?

She did not plan to subject herself to anymore of their interrogations.

"I think I'll go over and have a drink now. Would anyone like one? No? I'm sure—" she spoke hurriedly, distancing herself from the hurtful comments, and quickly slipped away before anyone could answer.

Not, however, before the fangs of Molly's old nemesis, in dark yellow taffeta, could claw out after her.

"Hey Molly, wudn't that you I seen at da crik a time back with that Powton fella?"

Despite ignoring everything else, for the life of her, Molly couldn't bear to hear her place called "the crik" or "Milcrik Purnd." With gritted teeth, she held back the teacher in her, dying to get the right "ee" and "o" sound out of the girl—if nothing else.

The other night she had to hold her breath to keep from correcting Alex, but in this girl's case she would have liked to slap the "long ee" in her mouth and force the "short o" down her throat. However, still not one for violence, she didn't; but Molly laughed aloud at the thought.

"What's so funny, Molly? Where's yo' beau? Couldn't get no one to bring ya?" Baring down on her teeth, the older girl smirked, savoring the last word.

Everyone in the cluster, including those who'd befriended Molly earlier, laughed loud and hard.

Regaining her composure, Molly headed to the other side of the ballroom. She stopped at a long table filled with every food imaginable. She wasn't very hungry at the moment, but she was extremely thirsty— considering the up and down events of the evening. She consoled herself with the thought that things could only get better from here, which they did.

Molly willed her sleek toned limbs to move through the ballroom with ease, as if she had always been attending festivals and mingling in society. She was in another place and time...imagining the clouds opening up to allow her true self to shine through. Through the open French doors leading out to the terrace, she felt a soft cool breeze slide against her warm flushed face.

"Yes, this is my time to take my place here on this delightful autumn evening," she told herself over and over again.

"Molly..." someone called, interrupting her blissful thoughts, "Is that you my dear?"

Aunt Minnie was standing behind her, in her regal gown with the lemon alabaster laced-bodice, smiling appreciatively at the exquisite vision the young girl made.

Molly's mother had worked all afternoon so she could have her hair draped up in glorious swirls with French ringlets hanging below each ear.

"My girl, you're like a beautiful princess...much too dignified for this group," Millicent added.

"Oh thank you, Aunt M..., I mean Ms. Millicent," she blushed, "I feel so complete now. Remember how we were sharing our hopes, and I told you about my plans...I have so many you see."

"And you should... and you can have even more than that...I suspect," the woman nodded knowingly.

Millicent Grandville eyed the wonderfully decorated banquet area, questioning Molly.

"Have you had any refreshments or am I too late? Has some handsome young man already seen to that?"

"Not yet, I just arrived a short while ago and have been taking in the exquisite décor. I was just heading out on the terrace to look at that spectacular evening sky."

"This is going to be one starry moonlit night. I'm sure of it," the older woman winked with an all-knowing look of youth revisited on such an evening.

Molly took it all in, dreamily agreeing, "Look... this moon *is* glimmering... these stars *are* twinkling..."

Standing under the twilight sky, both savoring the moment, someone touched Millicent's shoulder. She turned to find her niece Jean Jackson standing behind her. Although the hatchet was buried long ago, the aunt tried her best, these last few weeks, to avoid bringing Jean together with her cousin Lena.

For this reason, during her visit, Millicent regularly went to the Jackson estate to visit the other half of her family. Yet, she was glad to see Jean here tonight. It had taken her a while to get over Walter choosing her cousin—she believed—over her.

Molly, who'd turned around simultaneously to witness the owner of the slim well-manicured hand, mentally cringed, "...oh no, old maid sourpuss!"

Molly recalled seeing "the overdressed spinster" embroiled in a heated conversation with Ciaok when she first arrived. Hoping to avoid "fang-face," who not surprisingly, looked as bitter as she remembered, Molly lingered a moment behind the large entry doors before entering and greeting the friendly manservant.

Millicent now introduced her niece to Molly for what the aunt thought was the first time.

Molly, being polite for the occasion, nodded her head.

While Jean quipped, "We've met," without offering any formal gesture in return.

She then curtly added, "Unfortunately," and turned and walked away.

"I guess some things don't change," the older woman commented on her niece's rude behavior. Stinging from the blatantly obvious lack of civility displayed towards them both, Millicent explained some background of the situation and family history to Molly.

Millicent was surprised to hear the young girl comment, "Just think, the old man I used to talk to over the years, was Mrs. Neuman's uncle. I've lived here fifteen years and never, ever knew of all the relations running around this place."

With the evening still young, Molly and her "Aunt" Millicent stopped at the banquet table for refreshments. Before she could finish, Molly was invited to dance again and again by the many eligible young gentlemen who came from all over the state to attend the event.

Some glided with her to the traditional English waltzes, while others preferred the French courante dances of the newer Baroque Rondeau music. Several guests showed off one or two new struts introduced that year. Molly was surprised to attempt some steps she hadn't expected. She was glad she'd regularly practiced a variety of moves with Jake before he'd left.

She did miss him so much. Just yesterday, she had asked ma exactly where he'd gone, when he was coming back or maybe if they could visit him soon.

Looking at her partner now, this dance she was told, although not too enthused by its origins, used to be done on some of the old plantations where slaves competed with one another to win a piece of cake.

In order to please the plantation owners, many of the slaves added some movement from Irish jigs and reels. The best dances used exciting movements from all venues. Molly watched one couple in particular move from the front to the side and back, adding a swing of the arms and hips in a sway. Molly had never seen that exact dance before, although she'd practiced something like it on her own. She and her partner attempted to repeat that rhythm to a smooth sophisticated beat.

They moved together gracefully, yet boldly, to the music of the musicians. When they were done, everyone, including all the couples on the floor, clapped their approval.

The dancing mingled with the atmosphere and the drink caused Molly to feel a bit lightheaded. Since she didn't want to be too giddy before her waltz with Mr. Neuman's nephew, she went over to have a light meal before going back to the floor.

She decided to take her meal out on the terrace area near the balcony overlooking the garden path leading away from the house. Several people joined her as she sat taking in the moonlit view.

The Indian summer had come back momentarily and there was a light warm breeze in the air. The tall willow trees swayed back and forth bordering the rambling estate. The moonlight, she was sure, was reflecting off her "little lake" in the distance.

No one could have imagined tonight. Not after what happened just over a year ago. The whole county was stricken with that terrible fever and many of the people suddenly passed away. Those were terrible times. Along with everyone, Molly had tried to forget them, until Dr. Wagner brought it all back this evening. No, Molly and many others in attendance tonight could never forget. She recalled many of the people gone now.

During that time Grenada lost nearly 400 people in a town of no more than 2,000. Thinking about it, even now, Molly groaned, remembering how ma had given Jake and her so much of the "concoction" that they had to stay away from folks for fear of knocking people out with their scent. School was closed for over two months so that made it not so bad. When they'd ask ma why they had to take so much, she said they needed it to get what she called a very "strong constitution." Molly recalled, they even had to wear a poultice overnight, filled with various herbs. No one around knew what caused the sickness and had no real idea how to treat it.

The 'high-faluting' people in town and everyone else had to be what they called, "quarantined." Special trains came to town with nurses and equipment for only those folks who could afford them. But in our house, she recalled, people like Jake and me had to rely on our beloved ma to help us.

Even the prosperous Neumans, who were grateful their children had already gone to school up North, had gotten something from ma to help keep them from getting sick, because Mr. Neuman didn't want to leave the place. It seemed whatever the doctor was using in town wasn't working very well for most people.

Molly thought, I still don't know everything that went into ma's concoction, but I knew it had to be more garlic than most folks ate in a life-time— in every batch.

Even the mayor died that year. Most other, "high folks" did leave town before it got to them. Then, in early October, a cold spell finally put a stop to the dreaded sickness and spared the re-maining townspeople.

Whoa!

This was no time for the past. Molly shook her head, tossing her French ringlets from side to side, as if waking up from an unsuspecting nightmare. Why she went there, she wasn't sure, but she would not go there again, at least not to-night.

Tonight she could not think on Jake being gone, either. He'll be back soon. She knew it for sure.

Smoothing her furrowed brow and forcing a joyful smile to her perfectly made-up face, Molly pulled her thoughts back to the present.

Her smile was short-lived, however, as Mrs. Neuman slinked out onto the terrace.

Twenty-Three

"WEll, if it isn't Enola's little girl," Mrs. Neuman spoke, wearing a cryptic grimace, "What brings you to our home this evening?? I don't believe you were asked to serve tonight were you??"

After a few drinks, Mrs. Neuman was being even more disagreeable than usual. But as always with the lady of the house, Molly forbeared.

"I'm sure you've forgotten that I was to attend the festival as a guest, madam," Molly offered politely as she knew how.

"I'm sure I did, and I see you've gotten yourself a little frock for the occasion, too," the older women smirked, pinching at the clinched waist of Molly's gown.

As she pulled away from the unwanted touch, someone emerged from the shadows behind the slightly intoxicated missus.

This was an aberration that Molly hoped never to see again. Someone she hated more than anyone in her whole life. She relived how he had lunged at her throat in an attempt to strangle her that afternoon at the Neuman house not a few months earlier. Molly had never been utterly terrified of anyone, until that moment.

"I think the costume is quite breath-taking. And Lena you are being a bit brisk, even for you, my dear," his undeniable voice interjected.

Molly moved away from the direction of "that sound", "the presence" that rendered her speechless.

Petrified, she knew she must get away from him. This individual had threatened all that she had ever believed about herself. She had thought she was done with this reaction. But there was no explanation for what was taking place here. She didn't know what to say or if she could say anything.

And she wondered why this person was trying to defend her against Mrs. Neuman? Was this not the same madman who tried to attack her a few months ago? Hadn't he chased after her and tried to kill her?

Right after it happened, Mrs. Neuman had happily told Molly what he said he would do to her if he ever saw her again.

Had he forgotten what he said? Did she look so different that he didn't know who she was?

Now terrified a second time, Molly began to panic. Back inside her eyes scanned the room for someone to reach out to for help.

She tried to remain dignified, gliding alongside the windows through the French Provincially decorated ballroom, hoping to find someone.

Moving to the front hall, there was Ciaok by the doors. Unrecognizable, he held a strange far-away-sullen look which made Molly turn to avoid his usual assistance. No, she couldn't ask him. Her mind began to waver.

Wasn't this supposed to be special tonight? She seemed to recall. This was going to be the beginning of something, but all she could picture at this very moment was herself stripped down to torn rags, running away, hair twisted, struggling against a harsh wind with a whip at her back.

Molly's head was now whirling. She was beginning to lose consciousness, leaning to one side. She regained her balance in just enough time to fall into a red embroidered wing chair to the right of a small end table.

She quickly grabbed the edge of the table to pull herself back up. She willed herself to stand straight, strong and confident again. This shameful fear was not going to control her, she told herself.

"We meet again, uppity one," a voice behind her whispered softly in her ear, as she stood up.

Molly knew he had watched her every move. She deigned to use every bit of her own power, together with ma's instilled faith, and her ancestor's longsuffering ways to stand her ground this day.

As if redemption found her, Molly remembered she had promised the next waltz to young Dr. Wagner. With this, she attempted to excuse herself politely and turned in the direction of the ornate set of double doors leading from the front entry hall to the ballroom.

Having escaped Mrs. Neuman's cousin's scornful presence, noted as she turned and looked behind her, Molly slipped up the polished marble staircase before reaching the ballroom doors. She tightly grasped the mahogany banister for support as she made her way onto each step. She never looked back.

So many things were running through her mind at this moment; she couldn't be sure of anything. Molly only knew that she felt a deep foreboding that told her she must get away. An overwhelming dread she never experienced in all of her years here on the Neuman estate. Even her longtime discomfort in the presence of Mrs. Neuman didn't compare to this.

Molly didn't stop at the top of the stairway, but rushed past several closed doors to an open one at the far end of the hallway. The young girl stepped inside quietly closing the door behind her. She prayed no one noticed her come up-stairs or saw her go into one of the many family bedrooms.

Then, she thought, what does it matter, any-way? I'm busy cleaning and making beds in the-se rooms almost every day. So what if one of the family finds me, I've got a good excuse, she was convinced, wishing it was only a tongue lashing she had to fear.

Molly, trying to be herself again, didn't mind if they believed she had come up to make sure all was in perfect order, as long as she knew the truth. That hadn't changed, Molly told herself as she regained her composure. One person like Ms. Neuman or her hate-spewing cousin won't change it, either.

The truth being...soon she would be finished with this old life that made her subject to what seemed like every man, woman, and child on earth. Maybe things hadn't been as terrible right here, until now, but Molly knew she couldn't spend her whole life never venturing away from the Neuman estate.

Molly sank deep into one of two floral peach velvet chairs which added to the peaceful décor of the room. She remembered when Mrs. Neuman ordered them from somewhere across the ocean— London by way of Boston— she re-called. The madam was so thrilled about getting the pair of these specially made pieces to add to her collection of elegant things.

Wouldn't the madam have an absolute hissy fit, Molly laughed aloud at her next thought, if she could see me sprawled in one of her chairs right now?

Molly had to hold her breath to keep herself from giggling as she pictured the shocked expression and melodramatic outrage of Mrs. Neuman as she exploded at the sight of Molly smiling up at her from her beloved peach wing chair.

Moments had now passed, as Molly sat staring at nothing in particular. She then rose up and walked behind the chair to peer out of the red-draperied bay window. While looking out, Molly heard light footsteps on the polished marble in the hall, despite several rugs on the floor. Quickly, she tried to position herself behind the long, heavy drapes, pulling her ivory pumps as far back as her tiny, slim feet would go against the baseboard. She couldn't be sure that the tips weren't peeking out. She decided to remove her shoes, and place them on the sill so that she could stand hidden on her tip-toes.

The slight footsteps had stopped now. But she could not be sure that no one had seen her slip away up the stairs and down that long dark hall. Molly had not made a sound for several minutes. Breaking the absolute silence, she heard the door to the bedroom creak; then swing open.

Her eyes stretched wide open, her temples straining against the pins holding her French ringlets in place to each side of her head. Molly held her teeth firm, begging her limbs not to cringe with the old fear. She leaned forward slightly, but dared not peer from behind her covert hiding place, no matter what.

If she looked and was seen, she might be killed. If she looked and no one was there, she'd die anyway. Ma had always taught Molly not to play around with spirits. "It isn't for us to have nothing to do with what's beyond the naked eye. Those things be under the control of the man upstairs," she'd said. "And I'll have no tom foolery with the man downstairs, not in this house."

In the room now, Molly heard the tap of heels firmly pacing the hardwood floor. She was sure now, this was no spirit. The type of heels, though, male or female, she could not say. Each movement led their lightly carried pace toward the separate dressing area. Then she heard the dressing room doors side sideways and clothes rustling, as if being pushed aside, hangers taken down and put back in place. She could hear the doors to the dressing room slide back in place and the steps move closer to the canary, yellow canopy covered bed. Molly could clearly envision this person bending down to look beneath the white ruffled bed skirt.

The sounds now moved back toward the door leading to the hall, but that someone must have bumped the dresser because Molly heard a light thump followed by the melodious sounds of Mrs. Neuman's favorite French tune, "Claire De La Lune" drifting from her gold music box. After the music stopped, Molly pictured what was most likely the music box being placed back on the dresser. Several more footsteps, then the door leading from the bedroom creaked opened, then gently shut. Silence.

Molly held her breath, not willing to let out a sigh of relief, holding on to a thread hanging from the red lining of the curtains to help keep her focused. As she waited, grateful she hadn't been caught in Mrs. Neuman's bedroom; she pondered whether or not she had been followed from the ballroom at some point.

Molly waited a few more minutes before slipping on her shoes and emerging from behind the drapes. She tiptoed quietly towards the outer bedroom door. As her slim fingers reached to grasp the brass doorknob, Molly instantly yanked her hand back. The handle was painfully hot against her fingertips. Taking her wrap in her hand, she used it to open the door just slightly. Her eyes lit up with the glow emanating from frightful, red-hot flames as its fierce progression shot along the runner in the outside hall. Although still low, the smoldering red flames clouded the view of the imposing portrait lined walls. Smoke was now rising throughout the hallway and was slipping past the slight opening into the room as Molly held the door ajar. She quickly slammed the door shut, glad that it was designed to fit almost flush against the frame and the floor, and that she'd stopped the rising smoke from quickly entering the room. Searching her head for what to do next, Molly then pulled the quilt from the bed and pushed it on the floor against the door's bottom.

She knew the flames were now raging in the hall right outside Mrs. Neuman's room and she had to get out of this place, somehow. She could now hear voices shouting downstairs and the sound of people running. Outside of the windows, she heard someone calling for buckets of water to be brought and all available men to gather.

Molly crouched down, wrapping her arms around her slender body, gripping her shoulders in a state of shock and disbelief. Images swirled around her head; she was at the center of a whirlpool as each figure, one by one, descended into a dark pit below her.

Now trapped, she racked her weary brain to come up with something she'd done in her short life to deserve what was happening to her. Molly knew everyone said, "That there one don't know her place."

She could hear Mrs. Neuman tell ma, "The child has everything she ever deserved and was ever supposed to have in this life and more."

Even ma warned Molly that trying to get more from folks than they thought she rightly deserved, might be her ruination.

Molly now questioned aloud, "Did ma's God feel this way too?"

Her mind grappled with her fate as more smoke slipped into the room. Molly stumbled and fell as she backed away from the door

With her future and hope for anything, now eluding her, Molly still didn't want it to end for her right here.

Nauseously fighting a numbing feeling of utter hopelessness, she got up and forced her wobbly limbs towards the bedroom windows. After ripping off the lower half of her ball gown, she removed her shoes and stepped out onto the ledge.

Stoically, yet carefully, she made her way down from the second story, holding on to every frame slat and shutter she could, for support. Molly stretched out her leg onto a sturdy tree branch extending outside one of the other bedroom windows. Wrapping her arms around the strong limb, she clutched the tree and climbed down.

All the disheveled guests, men and women, were gathered outside on the side lawn of the house. The younger men were moving buckets, while others were just standing and staring with mouths open.

Those closest to that side of the house had watched Molly as she reached the outside ledge and descended down the cottonwood tree.

Like baby birds, people continued staring with their mouths agape. The sight Molly made as she stood before them in her bloomers—minus bustle, skirt and all— began to cause an even bigger stir than the fire. Many, despite the devastation before them, were outraged, especially the older ladies. In contrast, a few of the younger ones smirked and giggled, and some of the men thought it a good show.

One of the older women managed to ask, "Aren't you that Enola woman's chile, Mo- some-thing?"

At first, Molly had decided not to answer. Reeling from everything that had happened, she needed time to think.

"Answer her! "What the hell are you doing climbing out of the upstairs window," one of the men shouted, while everyone still marveled at the absence of the lower half of Molly's gown.

"Did I?" Molly managed to sputter question-ingly.

"You know, damn well you did," another man joined in, staring at Molly. He added, "And yo' indecent."

The first man queried, "You know what hap-pened? I heard that fire started up on the second floor, where you just climbed from it seems."

"Gentlemen, ladies," Molly responded with mock politeness, "I have absolutely no idea."

She walked off with a queenly strut, oblivious to the stares and the sight she made with her miss-ing attire.

"Just you wait r-at cheer. I'm gonna git Neuman over to talk ta ya," a simmering figure demanded, as he reached out to pull Molly back.

Fighting mad now, Molly snatched her arm up and away from the ominous man—backed off and fled.

She refused to stop as they shouted after her. She did not want to see Mr. Neuman, dressed like this. His opinion was the only one she cared about. How could she let him, of all people, see her this way?

Who cares what these other folks think. They never did anything for her, not one day in her whole life. But Mr. Neuman, he was different than anyone— even ma, she believed.

She took flight, never looking back. Molly knew they blamed her for starting the fire. That really didn't matter anymore, she told herself. Her life had now been ruined. And no one, not even Mr. Neuman, could do anything about it. Moving away from that fateful bedroom, she was ready to let her life take what she now understood was its predetermined course.

Molly now knew she would never be anybody. It was destined. She had no fight left in her. She might as well be dead.

Twenty-Four

Enola did not know what to do with the letter. After Molly left for the festival, before dark, she had decided to take the long walk to the postal office in Miserton to check for replies to her inquires about housekeeping positions up North. What she found waiting for her was something that would change her plans for the future. She ignored the foreboding she felt as she opened the correspondence.

She didn't want to give in to her worries and premonitions, because she didn't fancy herself superstitious, like some. But she did know that she could tell about things sometimes, and had some back and forth "talks" with her Creator when she got down to sleep at night. That's why even with her not following that "evil eye" shenanigans that some of the folks dabbled in, she did know that she had things revealed to her sometimes during those late night "talks."

The one last night, started with her questioning about Jake's leaving and then falling asleep before she got some direction. How could she explain what had happened after she fell asleep? She would not, and told herself that she could not—not to no one.

But, if forced to tell someone she would begin... "After I fell asleep, I dreamed I was somehow living in my mother's birthplace of Georgia, and I was wading through dark, murky waters. I saw my Jake just ahead, sitting near the side of the stream, staring off into the woods, like he was worried about something. He turned and saw me, and stood up and moved to the edge of the water. I called out for him not to jump in, but he did anyway. The water at his end was, at first, clear as crystal, but after he jumped in, it turned grey, then it got even darker, the same grimy color, like on my end. Finally, it turned black and thick as mud. I tried to reach him, but I couldn't swim no more, my arms and legs were moving, but I just stayed in that one place and had to cry out to my baby, watching the black sludge suck him down bit by bit, until only his hand was left and then I couldn't see him no more."

With everything in her, Evelyn ignored that vivid nightmare and took her time opening the mail in her trembling hand.

Holding off, in her troubled mind, she dwelled on how her two children were so special to her. But she knew that they were not special at all. But, like her, they were chosen. No different from others. Not overly good, not necessarily bad, just set apart. Like the Levites in the Good Book, following after those who came before them and leading the way for those to come after. All of mankind, even us handpicked ones, she told herself, suffer persecution; we love, hate, hurt, enjoy, mourn, cry and betray. But in our minds, within our heartfelt struggles to be free, the chosen know, through it all— nothing will last. So we do not fret. For we know it all be over soon—even time itself.

The letter finally reached up and took hold of her reluctant hand. Perspiration on her palms dampened the flap, as her moist fingers moved over it ripping the corner from left to right. The yellow paper on the inside was embellished with the same black fountain pen ink, in the same distinctive handwriting, as on the envelope. It was written by a stranger from up in Hardeman County, Tennessee who believed that he may have found her Jake— dead. The person was not positive, and wrote if she wanted to be sure that she had to come and identify the body.

Inside the envelope was a small newspaper clipping. The bold caption on the front side of the article stood out from the page, invoking the woman's frantic, unbelieving tears as she squinted to read the smaller print.

Found: *Young Negro with Broken Neck, Possible Lynching*

Body found hanging from trees near the IC Railroad depot, round the station hills and overlooking river. Tennessee Negro's fearful and plan to watch their ways, lest similar mishap befalls them or their kin. If your Negro kin is missing, come identify and claim this body. Will be kept for 7 days, if kin want to come or any white folks want to satisfy their curiosity.

Rereading the letter, enclosed with the hideous newspaper article, she understood that the letter writer and a few others there had seen Jake more than once, when they traveled to the mill, and had "talked to the boy" helping out with Mr. Neuman's books. Their townsfolk figured he probably had to be smart and might be important to somebody here. The man wrote, he knew from talking to Jake at the mill that his last name was McCray, so believed this was her boy, and saw to it that she got the letter. He ended the note writing she had only a few days to respond.

Enola held her head in her trembling hands. Her only son...her handsome, strong, gentle, loving child... He was the one she always believed would be safe. Always so mild, so unassuming, so very kind…he was.

"I don't believe it! Oh God…Why is there never an end to some folk's sorrow in this life?" She moaned. "My baby didn't deserve this; I will not accept it."

Even in her sorrow, she had to collect herself, in order not to make a scene. A Negro drawing attention was not acceptable, no matter what the circumstances. In addition, she was clearly part-Choctaw, and the sight of her made some Whites act with even more belligerence.

In her mind, all she was ever able to hold on to were the two children she was blessed with. Now, if this was true, it could be she only had the one left.

****

Arriving home, Enola was drawn to her son's cot on the other side of the big room. Pulling back the cover she eased her tired body into it— her "bed of mourning". Never one to embrace emptiness and sorrow, she was in agony. Once Molly got back she would have to be "ma" again. In the face of little hope, she could only be a pillar of strength for the one she was sure she had left. She must.

So many heavy memories weighed down her sturdy frame. But still she told herself, she would not fret. All would be over soon.

The lonely distraught woman buried her face in her son's hand-made checkered quilt, giving way to her long-held anguish and this most devastating blow. She allowed the tears to flow freely.

****

Molly's mother was asleep when she got in. Still in shock, she tore off what remained of her dress and climbed into her bed to sleep— forever. Destroyed, she remembered the bottom half of her dress, her beautiful ball gown and her exquisite new shoes— still in the bedroom at the Neuman estate where she removed them to escape. This night...so beautiful everything had been...it could have been perfect.

Once in bed, it didn't take long for the mental and physical pain to force her mind and ravaged body into a state of rest. She learned long ago how to free herself from reality.

A hard knock at the door awakened Enola. The door opened to Mr. Neuman and the sheriff. They had questions for Molly.

Her mother, confused and unaware of the time, still believed her daughter to be having the time of her life. Enola was shocked as both men explained what had happened that night.

"Oh my poor, poor baby," she cried.

"Her dream of such a wonderful 'coming out' at her first Autumn Festival. She is so different than most, you know, Mr. Neuman. So full of big hopes, loves life, people and...what she thinks they should be. She believes in fairness," her mother rambled.

The sheriff stopped her and again demanded to see Molly. "We'll come in, or she can come out here."

"She must be asleep, I'll wake her," her mother offered.

"But, I don't see how she will be able to help you, though. I can imagine that as bad as you feel, Mr. Neuman, sir, Molly feels just as bad."

"I know, Enola, we both know how Molly wanted to be a part of the festival this year," Mr. Neuman stood in agreement.

"Not only that, sir, yes that was very special for her, but she has always looked up to you. She sees you as a model for all the other folks around here. She wants you to be pleased with her." Enola almost added, "...to make you happy."

The sheriff cut in, "Get her now."

Enola moved painstakingly across the long, now gloomy room and into the larger back area. Several moments later, Molly emerged.

The girl's eyes held an empty blank stare.

From the depths of that emptiness came, "Mr. Neuman, sheriff...May I help you?"

"Yes, you can girl," the sheriff jumped right in, "I understand you was seen coming out of a second flo' window near where the fire started last night. Can you explain that?"

"Of course, I had to go upstairs. When I went to come down, I couldn't get out. A fire had started in the hallway, or somewhere. So I had to climb out of the window." Molly answered stoically, as if in a trance.

The sheriff responded, "Why was you upstairs? Was there somebody else up there with you?"

She responded lifelessly, "I believe someone followed me up the staircase, so-o-o...," she seemed to emerge from her trance, "...yes, there was someone else up there!"

"Did you question anyone else!?" she asked the sheriff, almost like her old self.

Agitated by the counter-questioning, he responded harshly, "None of yo' business."

He then added, looking over at Mr. Neuman, "The other guests say you was the only one seen coming from that second flo'."

"But I *told* you someone else must have followed me up. I heard someone rummaging around and footsteps," Molly now recalled.

"Who?" The sheriff asked unbelievingly.

"I don't know, but they were in the same room as I was in," she responded warily.

"Yo' telling me someone followed you up...they was in the same room wit you... but you didn't see 'em," he mocked.

"I couldn't...," Molly continued.

"Was you blindfolded at the time," the sheriff laughed cruelly.

"No," Molly answered, and then paused.

"I was hiding," she responded with finality.

"And pray-tell what reason would you be hiding?" The sheriff responded, losing all patience with the girl, "And from somebody you say you never even saw!?"

Mr. Neuman broke in, "Wait Molly. I still don't understand what you were doing upstairs... and hiding, you say? You were invited to be a part of the festival. You shouldn't have been up there working nor hiding from anyone."

Mr. Neuman would never understand. Molly wasn't even sure herself who it was she was hiding from. If she told him she was hiding from Mrs. Neuman's cousin, the man could just deny he was up there.

Thinking she should reflect some more before she answered again, Molly methodically went over the details in her mind.

She now wondered if she really cared what happened anymore. All she did know was that she did feel some responsibility for what happened to Mr. Neuman's house.

He looked utterly drained and disappointed— she noted— standing there near the little window with the early dawn light resting on his lean almost haggard-looking face.

Ready to answer, Molly pleaded, addressing herself now to the mill owner, "I don't know sir, but I didn't start that fire. Please never think that I would do something like that to you... or anybody else."

"Molly, I would never—not ever—believe that you would on purpose. But you must admit, it

216

could have been an accident," Mr. Neuman spoke softly, looking for confirmation in the young girl's eyes.

"I'd tell you, sir...if it happened that way, but that is not so," Molly defended herself, "I just don't know what happened. I wish I could help you, but I can't."

The sheriff seemed to have had enough of the bantering back and forth.

"Help us!" He bellowed loudly, "Why, I held my tongue long enough, out of respect fo' Mr. Neuman here. But I sez, you are one l'l scalawag and I'll be gol-derned if you sho' ain't a dang liar to boot."

Listening to the sheriff break into full dialect, Walter knew what was coming next, so he demanded... "Let's go!"

He almost pulled the sheriff away from the open doorway.

"Neuman!" The sheriff demanded in return, "Don't you want this here thang solved? You want the culprit that almost burned down yo' house- don't ya?"

"Yes, I surely do," the now angry mill owner assured him, "but we've spent enough time here."

With the early morning breaking through, Molly looked on as the two men pulled back and turned away onto the dimly lit path. Before walking off, the sheriff threw her a parting look that promised that he wasn't finished with her and would be back.

She didn't want to talk to the sheriff, Mr. Neuman, or anyone else about what happened last night. She never wanted to talk to anyone about it ever again. She just wanted to get away...to think.

Looking at her daughter Enola wasn't sure what to do. Although last night must have been tragic for her, Molly's behavior right now was even more so. Enola had never seen her daughter like this. She didn't want to tell anyone else for fear that they'd use the way Molly was now behaving as evidence of guilt.

Molly stared blankly at the white-washed walls beside her now rumpled bed. Her attention turned to a lone cinder sticking up from the plank floorboards. She reached down to pick it up.

It wasn't supposed to be like this... in despair she communicated in her mind to whomever from above had been responsible for her current fate.

She recalled the afternoons of "proper" training with ma.

Might as well say "mama," even "mammy" for all the good being proper will do now... she concluded.

Studying the sliver of wood, Molly looked up again to see her mother staring at her with a sorrowful expression that Molly didn't recognize. She wondered if her mother was thinking the same as everyone else...like they always thought.

"…should be what God meant you to be," or, "One day yo' ways will get you into trouble… you'll see," old Mr. Richmond had said.

Was he there tonight? She wondered.

"Better to be no-count," *like this little piece of wood*, "than always wishing for something you can never get," she could hear them shouting at her over and over again.

Enola reached out as she watched her daughter place her hands over her ears as if to shut out some loud noise. Extending warm, soft arms around her "beautiful baby," she rocked her, gently humming to soothe her pain.

Molly, now oblivious to the comforting touch, could not shut out her thoughts.

How could she forget, when sometimes at night she'd dream that she had been transplanted from somewhere else. She had read about people in France and England in some of her schoolbooks and always felt her mannerisms and tendencies had more to do with the heroines in those novels than those around her. Molly knew she wasn't a "patient," still she felt that although she had actually never known those people, she was more like her "night visitors" than anyone she had known face to face in the daylight.

High hopes for a bit of that other life, at times, had given her a feeling of total uninhibited freedom and imagined acceptance. This was all she ever really wanted. That independence and recognition, she'd believed, should have been made complete this fateful night.

Molly past, present, and future would have somehow intertwined in a way she knew was true, but could explain to no one.

But what had happened? She wasn't sure. The years spent on the Neuman estate with ma, the Neumans, in this town, with those people— all had brought Molly to this sorrowful moment.

Was the dream, no matter how badly trampled upon, still worth having? How could it be? She wondered. It had always been reality to her, much more than the things others said and did to her could have ever been.

Those things she'd seen, heard, and things purposefully left out— all were now reflected in the sad hazel brown eyes of the tear-stained face in the box-shaped looking glass.

Accepting *that* girl staring back at her now— as she was, with no hope—could Molly do that?

Twenty-Five

Walter Neuman paced the floor of his bedroom. He was grateful that the fire was quickly contained and confined only to the hallway and one bedroom in the east wing. Rumor already had it that half of his second story was burned beyond repair, but that was not the case.

He was surprised that so many people were in such a tension-filled state, not over the damage to his own home, but that their long awaited weekend had been ruined. Since each year's festival was always their highlight, many told him that the rest of the year—even though the holidays were just around the corner— was lost to them. This was something that he just could not bring himself to understand nor would he accept responsibility for. He refused to be an overseer of another person's hopes and wishes.

He and his wife were the only ones who put up all the money for planning, food, decorations, and extra help— not just the costumes. But Walter did realize that many put up quite a bit for their clothing, in comparison to what they actually owned.

Walter couldn't deal with Lena now, he thought to himself. She was still in bed, thank goodness. She took that headache powder of hers late last night and would be out until the afternoon. She would never see the incident in the same light as he did. The sheriff's investigation and getting the house re-done would not be enough for her. He knew that she would demand that someone pay personally for this devastation of her work, her image, of this perfect weekend that was to be hers to command.

Walter walked down to the furthest end of the long hallway. The walls were charred black, the rugs completely burned away, but the marble floors were spared.

As he turned to go back, he looked down along the undamaged marble and saw something lying there standing out among the ashes. He picked up what appeared to be a solid gold ladies pendant. It was in an area near a wall that was barely scorched by the fire. At first he didn't recognize it, but then he remembered the one that his wife used to wear years ago.

This looked exactly like it. He dusted off the delicate snake-like chain, placed it in his jacket pocket and continued down the hall through his wife's adjoining dressing room. Walter quietly entered her bedroom as she slept. He opened one of her jewelry boxes, then another and found that her pendant was sitting inside, golden and shining up at him.

Feeling relieved, but with some guilt over the suspicion that had previously entered his head, Walter now asked himself how could the exact pendant be laying against the marble in the hallway?

He was totally beside himself now. Walter wanted to wake his wife so they both could get to the bottom of this, but he knew that would be a mistake. They had been at odds so much lately. Undecided as to his next move, Walter sat down in one of the custom-made wing chairs near the draped windows and waited.

****

"Molly," Enola whispered softly. "Honey, it's alright. It's going to be all right. I don't care what nobody says."

Blaming herself, Enola continued, "I wish I'd left when I had the notion to. We'd be long gone by now."

Having chosen her destiny, Molly decided to consol her mother— letting all things proper fall by the wayside, "Now ma don't go blaming yourself. Anyways whatever happens to me... well, ain't nobody to blame but me. I didn't know when to stop. But I do now. Things is going to be different with me from now on mama."

"What are you saying, girl?" Enola had felt a strange sensation run through her at Molly's tone and temperament. "And why are you talking like that? You of all people said you didn't want nobody and you meant it...forcing you to talk this way."

"Well, things have changed now mama. You're looking at the new Molly. Just think of me as "Mo." Yes, that's what old Mr. Richmond and the others call me. A non-descript gal who should bother no one. Asks for nothing and offers nothing in return. Someone who just exists by staying out of everybody's way."

"Girl, I won't have you talk like that. Stop it, now!" Enola demanded of this shadow of her once opinionated daughter.

"I can't, ma. I am being me, now. My life will always be here. This way, I will stop trying to take some non-existent path to nowhere. I vow to never forget my place!"

And with this proclamation Molly shot out the door and down the dirt road before her mother could stop her.

****

A short distance away, after almost collasping from exhaustion after the night's dramatic ending, Mrs. Neuman finally woke up to her husband's questions about the mysterious necklace. It seemed that her Aunt Millicent had several of the same necklaces made for Lena and her cousins Jean and Marie many years ago.

Backtracking, Walter recalled that the Jacksons were at the festival last night. He hadn't noticed anything stranger than usual about their behavior.

With questions, Walter called downstairs for Ciaok to come up. When asked about the Jacksons, the man spoke up.

"Mr. Neuman I really did not want to bring this to you. I was concerned, but I did not feel it was my place to say anything. I have not been myself for the last few years, so I thought who am I to point a finger at anyone else?"

In detail, he described a time later in the evening when "Miss Jean" had gone upstairs and had not emerged downstairs at the festival for quite a while. He was concerned since Mrs. Neuman said that her cousin had been in the hospital for over a month for some undisclosed illness. So he started up to check on her just as she finally came down. He asked if there was anything he could do for her, she dismissed his offer of assistance with an abrupt, "hardly."

Walter didn't want to approach the sheriff with any suspicions unless he was absolutely certain. In addition, whoever the culprit was, if it was an accident, Walter wouldn't feel right pressing charges. Even his wife's eccentric clan despite how estranged they were from everyone, deserved a fair shake.

Remembering her deep regret, Walter suddenly felt compelled to check on how Molly was getting along. He still had a hard time tying her to the fire in any way— accident or not. But the sheriff seemed to be completely focused on her. No matter how she protested, he knew many people wanted this particular girl to be brought to some kind of justice. She was an easy scapegoat to blame this on.

Mr. Neuman hurried, picking up his step. From a distance, he saw the sheriff approaching the young girl's front door.

****

Molly tore down the dirt path, through the avenue of spruce and pines, towards the willow trees to the only place she ever really felt totally free.

Out of breath, she stopped short and fell down on the ground under the early morning sky, her mind taking over.

Just a part of the landscape, I am. Like that pine back there. Its roots stay in one place, life touches it, it can't touch back. It's beautiful, tall, mighty, strong, wretched, cold, clinging, still.

Sometimes, is there a way out? Probably not.

Become a mountain, maybe. All rests on how high the great hill reaches above — melancholy mounds, ascending mightily. Or be a canyon, how deep down the bed must cower—a fortress of floors descending below.

Should one go up, down or even around? Either way, one will have to make a place... somewhere.

A place to hide. Camouflage. Become invisible. Unnoticed.... Secure... Safe.... Finally.

The late autumn winds had picked up earlier that night. The trees, now violently swaying back and forth, beckon Molly on to safety. It had turned frightfully cold and gray that morning. In the misty daylight the tall willows stood naked, missing their leaves. It was so unlike the day she remembered sitting at this same spot only a few months ago. Then, Molly had thought her life was over only because ma was thinking to move. That seemed so long ago now. Strange, how being able to live here, was so important to her then.

"I guess it's too late to move now," she cracked, as she tried to laugh at her own feeble attempt to make light of all of this, as the winds began to die down and early morning fog rolled in.

"At least this quiet spot is as perfect as ever." She thought, "Some things never change, even without the leaves."

Molly remembered swimming with Jake and the other children. Then the day she and Alex first came here and how she used to study her reflection in this, her very own pond. How she played teacher with the sharecropper's younger children. Molly had always claimed this place as her own.

She wondered what Mr. Neuman's children and Jake were doing up North now. She missed them all, but no comparison to her brother Jake. Maybe this night would have never happened if Jake had stayed. He was her rock, and knew how to keep her out of trouble. Deep down, she really didn't understand how he could leave her and ma, even though she said she did.

She continued to reminisce, convinced that the best part of her life was spent here, including practicing her dancing for the Autumn F....

"Anyone over there?" someone called.

She heard the voice calling in the near distance. Her first instinct, after last night, was to run. Molly needed to protect her place where only good things happened. Here held the best part of her life. She would not let anyone inflict sadness and pain on her—not here.

Molly jumped up; throwing off the broken twigs she'd unconsciously placed over her legs, and ran away from her oasis into the forest area towards the Jackson place.

"Hey—who's over there?" The voice called again.

The frightened young girl, not thinking rationally anymore, pushed through the darkness blindly fleeing her fate. Her mind raced. She pictured the cousin. Could it be him again, Mrs. Neuman's cousin? It sounded more like that sheriff. He said he'd be back. She ran faster.

The fog, dense and heavy now, blocked her view so she was unable to make out whom or what could be tracking her through the trees. Escaping their pursuit, Molly's foot gave way, dragged, then stumbled over a broken branch that had fallen to the ground and blocked her way. She landed hard against rough jagged rocks underneath. She knew it was over now. She could hardly put her weight on her ankle, much less run. Fear took over.

Wincing, her eyes half-closed, Molly stretched out and felt the ridged frame of the old oak with its thick branches, reaching out for the morning light. She was half-conscious now, fighting the terrible pain, the descending clouds choking her, forcing her to relive that day—the first time fear overtook her.

It was when she first got the illness, the one that made her foot give way like it did just now. That day over eight years ago, when she knew for a fact she saw something strange, over six feet tall, with a white covering standing at the foot of her bed, when she woke one night. She called out to ma, praying it was somehow her, but the body just stood there. Molly was half asleep, and it was the middle of the night, so she wasn't sure that it wasn't a nightmare. *I must be dreaming*, she had told herself. So she called again, "ma, ma..." Nothing. Then fright took over, and Molly slid her head, body and every part of her under the cover into a rigid ball, with eyes shut tight, to dispel the nightmare or force sleep to come between herself and whatever stood at the foot of her bed. It all came back now, flooding her with natural and supernatural terror.

"Got to pull myself up." she struggled aloud, "Got to come out of this."

Thrashing about, fighting to stay coherent, tears began to stream down her dirt- stained cheeks. The fragile girl winced again at the stabbing pain in her ankle. She desperately tried to cart herself out of harm's way. Holding her throbbing limb, slightly dragging it, she spotted a newfound security, behind the wide, welcoming frame of the nearby, old oak tree.

"Come back." The voice, closer now, somehow sounded familiar.

It's a trick, I know it is, her mind rambled.

With her back to the impending danger, she crotched low behind the open covering, closed her eyes, and said her prayers. She could hear the broken twigs crackling as "the end" moved closer to her. It was now only a few feet away. She could hear "it" coming slowly toward her.

Molly placed her head down between her shivering knees and flinched like a wounded animal, as a large hand came down on her trembling shoulder.

The touch was unexpectedly gentle, not grabbing at her or trying to hurt her as she had feared.

"It's over," the voice said.

****

In her anguish, she did not recognize the voice of the person calling her or standing over her at that moment.

"Molly, look up. It's okay to look up," the voice said.

Somewhere in her mind, Molly felt that this was not who she believed it was. It wasn't someone she could trust, who cared for her, and whom she cared for.

Remember the foot of my bed, she braced herself, waiting, before lifting her head and opening her eyes.

I don't want nothing like that. Don't want anything to do with it.

"Open your eyes, I won't hurt you", the voice cracked with emotion.

She could now decipher the familiar tone, which added, "You don't have to be afraid. Not anymore."

With extreme caution, she very carefully lifted her pounding head away from her knees and turned her tear-soaked face towards that of the silhouette standing over her.

"M-M-Mr. N-Neuman. Mr. Neuman, Mr. Neuman she cried over and over again." Tears were streaming down her face. "Is there anyone with you this t-t-time? Anyone to c-c-come and t-t-take me away?" She begged not.

"No one. Not ever." He swore loudly.

Distraught himself, Mr. Neuman bent down and placed his arms around the shoulders of the slight melancholy child he'd watch grow up over the years.

"I-I thought you were...oh I don't know who I thought you were, but I knew everyone was against me. It didn't matter who was after me. I had to run."

Feeling some relief, momentarily, Molly began to spill out her own suspicions about who could have started the fire at Mr. Neuman's house. She told him that she believed someone had followed her upstairs. Molly thought it could be, she was sorry to say, Mrs. Neuman's cousin, explaining how he'd threatened her. She believed he may have started that fire to kill her.

"I swear sir, I swear it was not me," she willed him to believe her.

Molly was taken aback when Mr. Neuman told her the reason he'd come to find her. He explained he may have found out who was really responsible for what happened last night.

"I would never have suspected Mrs. Neuman's other cousin, Miss Jean," Molly sat wide-eyed, wiping her face with Mr. Neuman's handkerchief and taking in the story in detail.

"I know, why would anyone? We're still not sure if it was an accident or not.

While looking for you, I ran into the sheriff and told him the whole story. He is over there at their house now asking questions."

"So he was still after me, in a way," Molly concluded.

"How do you mean?" He asked.

"If he had walked over this way to get to Miss Jean's house, he may have run into me. If I'd seen him, I never would have stopped, even with this ankle," she laughed nervously, wincing but not caring about the pain now.

The weary pair smiled gently at one another as the old Molly emerged again for a moment.

As the early morning sunlight broke through the misty gray fog, Molly took a long deep breath, still holding Mr. Neuman's handkerchief against her slightly bruised, tear-stained face.

Twenty-Six

"You have to tell her," he pleaded once again.

"I never wanted her to know, especially not now, let her have her happiness in this life. It would confuse her even more," she assured him.

"She has to know before long, Enola. How can someone not tell her? I thought John wouldn't see her again, but now that Minnie is taking her to Boston, they'll be together again. He's her first cousin, we have to tell her."

"Walter, nobody understands how it was for us back then; how do you expect Molly to accept it now?"

"Lena has had her suspicions for years," he continued.

"After filing for divorce and taking the children up North for so long, we both believed our life together was over. I always loved my wife, but I never believed she would decide to come back. Since then she's tried to make life miserable for you, even though I never really told her the truth."

"I understand her hurt," Enola sympathized, "She obviously knows now. I don't think she suspected anything years ago. That was my only saving grace when my husband, your nephew, died young. He never knew. Along with Jake, Molly was his, as far as he knew, and for that, I am so very grateful. He was a good man. It was wrong, what we did. Even though you know we never meant to hurt anyone, I repented a long time ago."

"Maybe I should have owned up to everything, but Lena was gone— gone for good she said— and Molly will never be anyone's mistake," he assured her.

"Look Walter, I plan to move anyway, once Molly gets back. You know that's the only way it can ever be. It's a wonder these nosey folks around here haven't told her something already. Heaven knows they suspect and have hinted as much. She's so very headstrong, but she's delicate, still. I'm afraid for her. I just can't tell her."

"But, my nephew, John..." Walter began.

Enola stopped him, "Walter, she has no interest in him and you said your sister is aware of the situation. She can keep them apart.

"Yes, I know Ms. Granville lives near your sister's people," she continued adamantly, "but Boston is a big place and the best one right now for her. I pray she never learns the truth."

Enola's thoughts turned to her train ride up to   Hardeman County, Tennessee scheduled the day after Molly's departure. She had told no one about Jake, although she could barely stand under the strain. She prayed that those folks were wrong; that the pitiful dead soul was not her Jake, and that she would never have to share her wrenching pain with her now fulfilled daughter.

Twenty-Seven

Life was changing for the better, but Molly still had a few mysterious unknowns she needed to wrap up before she would fully move forward. She had arrived home feeling a lot older. She also had even more determination under her belt to get to the bottom of things around there, despite everything that had just happened. Molly had questions for her mother, Mr. Neuman, and almost anyone else who would listen, about every aspect of the mysterious strategic parts, missing from sketchy tales she'd heard or was told.

Presently exhausted, and still limping quite a bit from her ordeal, she hobbled towards the welcoming front door of the familiar gray shanty where Millicent Grandville was waiting anxiously for her.

Learning of how Molly was found that misty gray morning, Mrs. Grandville came over and graciously offered to take the young ingénues back to Boston with her for an indefinite period of time, and a well-deserved extended rest. Enola hesitantly agreed that this hiatus would be the best thing for Molly after all the turmoil.

Judging from the newly etched lines across her brow, Aunt Minnie still worried over Molly's terrible ordeal in the woods and her noticeable ankle strain, and now witnessed Molly's slight cough as she dragged through the battered weather-worn door. Hiding her concern, the older woman slipped a mask over her urge to grab the tortured child and never let go, replacing the inclination with a show of tough love, reprimanding the girl, "Don't try to create any more hindrances 'pretty one', you promised to stay with me for a good while.

"Without a doubt, my girl," she went on, "you will get to see your very first snowfall this winter. You'll surely have a good look and feel of at least one big fluffy covering for Christmas."

Molly had heard about the white, cold, icy stuff, but had wondered if she'd ever get to see it.

Aunt Minnie's clear description of snowflakes, glitter and tinsel, sledding and making angels in the snow filled Molly with even more anticipation of the unknown she'd yet to experience.

"Aunt Minnie, even if I caught the dreaded yellow fever, I'd still find a way to go," Molly half-joked.

"Well, that's good," she laughed, "because your mother thinks it's a fine respite, and I did ask her to come too, but she feels she should stay here and take care of the place. Though, she promised, she will make plans to come visit you for a while in the spring."

After enduring two more days, filled with hurried preparation, the kindred pair was set to escape by means of one of Walter Neuman's carriages and the next passenger train leaving from the Grenada's Illinois Central Railroad Station heading north.

When Enola confided that the train conductor might try to make Molly ride second, even third class, Millicent Grandville deftly pointed out that she was now in charge.

After Molly's ordeal, Enola cried, she sure couldn't stand the thought of her baby traveling alone in an open car with a wood seat, one washroom, and toting her own food with everyone looking at her.

"When you look different from most everybody around, that don't help much either," she added.

Millicent assured her again, "Not even second.

We'll just see about that. Don't you worry."

More excited than ever, Molly gave her word to ma that she would not stay for an extended season or too long-a-spell, definitely not past the next winter. Especially, she told herself, since she still had her one and only suitor still living in Grenada. She had big plans for them both; she'd shared with him, one's that included so many changes that could not be held off for much longer.

Millicent Grandville had big plans for the both of them, too—Molly and her.

"Since so many of my things smell like smoke these days, I didn't need to pack much," the older woman quipped. "This will give us a legitimate reason to shop a long while at the clothing stores as soon as we get back to Boston."

She spoke freely, gently squeezing Molly's hand. "Together, we will get to display our true selves, pretty one."

****

Their departure hour had definitely arrived, sealed by Alex stopping in and promising to wait for Molly. They both agreed to finish their plans and work on them together. The young man reassured Molly that he really did want to fit into what she called her "elaborate plan for their lives."

When confronted with the necklace, Mr. Neuman came and told them, Jean confessed to starting the fire, but said that it was nothing but an accident. She was afraid no one would believe her, so she said nothing about poking around upstairs uninvited. Since she felt many believed that she never got over her feelings of rejection by Walter Neuman years ago, she stated that she knew they would be skeptical of her story.

She had used the opportunity of the Autumn Festival, she reluctantly added to her confession, to satisfy an "old maid's" curiosity and rummage through several of the stately upstairs rooms. She rushed off after she knocked down one of the wall candles over in the hall, and couldn't put it out, as she tried to sneak back downstairs unnoticed.

"I don't know if I believe it was just an accident or not," Neuman submitted with a long sigh, "but I'll just leave it up to the sheriff."

Consciously drifting away from the others, Molly and her beau embraced and said their goodbyes under the watchful eyes of her mother, Aunt Minnie, and Mr. Neuman.

"Oh, before I forget," Molly coughed, and then turned to her mother, "No talk of moving ma, right? You'll be here when I get back?"

Enola hugged her persistent child one moment longer, and then added, "I'll do my best, my girl. Okay, I promise I'll be here when you get back."

"Well that's that," Aunt Minnie proclaimed. "Are you ready for the shining carriage to take you away?"

The Neuman's fancy black carriage was waiting for them in front of the house.

Molly cleared her scratchy throat, and then rang out, "Aunt Minnie I am so-o ready."

"Girl, that throat of yours—I've listened to you cough one time too many these last two days. If the herbs don't stop it by the time we get to Boston, I'm taking you straight to a doctor," she whispered so as not to alarm the others.

Molly nodded in agreement to anything right now.

Her mind wistfully turning to those she was leaving behind; she reluctantly waved goodbye to her beau, her ma, and her longtime benefactor Mr. Neuman as she stepped up into the gleaming black coach.

As she rode away, Molly's eyes lingered on the shining faces of her loved ones. She fondly studied their every facet as they went back and forth between talking and waving goodbye in her direction. She wondered what they were discussing, even now.

Sunlight leading the path, glimpsing her dream ahead, Molly still hadn't forgotten all the questions she held for those behind, even Jake, when he got back.

Nevertheless, dispelling haunting echoes of the past, she took a long satisfying breath, knowing with time she'd be back to change things.

Looking around, she closed her eyes to hold back the tears, and then used the fingertips of her gloves to dab the tiny droplets seeping from the corners, before reaching for an embroidered, white handkerchief in her handbag.

Her eyes slightly veiled, she peered far ahead to the edge of the pond across from the mill. There stood a mirage? ...Her imagination? A familiar shape, standing erect— was the old oak tree. Its thick, sturdy trunk supporting strong branches connected to swaying thinner limbs, holding on to the many tiny stem-like twigs at the ends. Reaching out to her, standing tall, simulating the waving arms of her present day loved ones, was this haunting silhouette; the big oak tree with the wind carrying its arms to and fro.

They had all come together to say goodbye.

She was positive that tree had been there forever waiting for this day to arrive, and now she had ma, Mr. Neuman, Alex, Aunt Minnie, sharing this moment with her. Later others will come and lead the way—moving everything forward, woven together into the tapestry of time. She could not separate them nor would she ever try. All were a part of her, the good times, and the bad; connected and cared for, watched over, always— by the Creator of time itself.

Misty-eyed, she lifted her slim, lace-gloved hand for a final goodbye. From the carriage window, she was close enough now to glimpse her

reflection in the "little lake" she no longer needed —yet no less loved—as the coach passed en
route to the station for the afternoon train.

****
**

Epilogue

The sheriff decided not to press charges against Jean Jackson for starting the fire on the night of the Autumn Festival. It could not be proven that it was not an accident and since she was related to the Neumans, he did not want to go any further into what he considered a family matter.

Enola visited Hardeman County, Tennessee and could not identify the poor battered soul who lay in front of her. She contributed along with some others a small sum to have him buried in an unkempt Negro cemetery. She vowed that she would find a way to get in touch with her Jake because she knew this was not him. Even if she could not be sure, she knew in her heart that it was not her boy. She continued to search for him, hoping he didn't get off the train before arriving North.

Mr. Neuman continued to work at his prized mill and look for a way to keep he and Mrs. Neuman on good terms, especially after she became bedridden for many months after the fire occurring in her grandiose home by a cousin of hers, which made it even more horrible, in her mind. He continued to make up for past mistakes by focusing day by day, step by step, on moving Grenada, Mississippi towards becoming a place where any man of any race, creed or color could live freely.

Molly found Boston to be everything she had hoped for. She met many exciting people of all races, and those who, like her, enjoyed the opportunity to live and be treated as human beings. She had come to adore and depend on Aunt Minnie, who included Molly in every aspect of her life and many events. But Molly missed home. Not so much Grenada County, but her loved ones. Her ma could not be replaced by anyone, and then there was Alex. She would be on her way home before too long, maybe sooner than expected.

Afterword

Thanks to you, my loving family for allowing me time over the years to get my story down on paper. … through all of life's mundane, sometimes sad, and wonderful changes and interruptions.

Also, thanks to those who took the time to read my story.   I am very grateful.

References in order of appearance:

Farming (http://www.anokaareachamber.com /farming1860.htm

A look at the North and the South during the Jackson Era American Diversification

(http://www.schonwalder.org/USHistory/usstory2.htm

"The Choctaw Trail of Tears" The Choctaw Nation of Oklahoma, by Chris Watson, 1999

http://www.thebicyclingguitarist.net/studies/trailoftears.htm#top

History of Yellow Fever, "History of Grenada County," http://www.rootsweb.com/-msgrenad/grenyfvr.htm

Godley's Ladies Book (http://www.history.rochester.edu/godeys/)

Yellow Fever "History of Grenada County," http://www.rootsweb.com/-msgrenad/grenyfvr.htm.

Water Wheel
http://en.wikipedia.org/wiki/Water_wheel#Hydr
aulic_wheel

From Revolution to Reconstruction-An Outline
of American History.
(http://www.let.rug.nl/usa/H/1954uk/chap5.htm

"Time Line of The Civil War, 1863" Joanne
Freeman, Encyclopedia of American History by
Richard B. Morris.,
(http://rs6.loc.gov/ammem/tl1863.html)

Choctaw-
http://www.angelfire.com/realm/shades/nativeam
ericans/choctaw.htm

About the Author

Kay Carroll leads a quiet, yet busy, life teaching and motivating teens on strategies to develop and pursue personal and career goals. She lives with her husband and three children in northern Illinois.

Made in the USA
Monee, IL
08 March 2023

29422732R00146